THE ONCE AND FUTURE CANADIAN DEMOCRACY

The Once and Future Canadian Democracy

An Essay in Political Thought

JANET AJZENSTAT

McGill-Queen's University Press
Montreal & Kingston · London · Ithaca

© McGill-Queen's University Press 2003
ISBN 0-7735-2658-7 (cloth)
ISBN 0-7735-2659-5 (paper)

Legal deposit fourth quarter 2003
Bibliothèque nationale du Québec

Printed in Canada on acid-free paper.

McGill-Queen's University Press acknowledges the support of the Canada Council for the Arts for our publishing program. We also acknowledge the financial support of the Government of Canada through the Book Publishing Industry Development Program (BPIDP) for our publishing activities.

National Library of Canada Cataloguing in Publication

Ajzenstat, Janet, 1936–
    The once and future Canadian democracy: an essay in political thought / Janet Ajzenstat.

Includes bibliographical references and index.
ISBN 0-7735-2658-7 (bnd)
ISBN 0-7735-2659-5 (pbk)

1. Canada – Politics and government.
2. Democracy – Canada.   I. Title.

JL159.A49 2003   320.971   C2003—902967-0

Typeset in 10/12 Palatino by True to Type

To Sam,
for science, art, and music

Contents

Preface ix

PART ONE LIBERALS AND ROMANTICS

1 *Prenez Garde!* 3
2 Beyond Right-Centre-Left 10
3 The Evil Futures 20

PART TWO GETTING TO DEMOCRACY

4 What Romantics Say 33
5 Are We There Yet? Liberal Arguments 40
6 Why Historians Can't Put a Date to Democracy 48
7 What Did the Fathers Say? 60
8 The Monarchical Element 70
9 Parliament: The Talking Shop 81

PART THREE BRINGING IN THE FUTURE

10 Last Train from Right-Centre-Left 93
11 Romantic Ideas: George Grant 102
12 Romance in a Democratic Clime 116
13 The Romantic Artist in Her Lonely Garret 127
14 The Three Deaths of the Canadian Constitution 137

Sources 149
Index 189

Preface

This book asks Canadians to abandon the political scientist's standard explanatory model with its three historical categories: conservatism, liberalism, and socialism and to adopt instead the distinction, familiar in the arts and in philosophy, between classicism and romanticism. It argues that Canadian political history and our politics today reveal a tension – a quarrel if you will – between the classicism of the European Enlightenment and the romanticism of the Counter-Enlightenment.

I am indebted to two authors especially. The first is Isaiah Berlin, whose lectures on the Counter-Enlightenment were delivered in 1965 and published in 1999 as *The Roots of Romanticism*. The second is Judith Shklar. In *After Utopia: The Decline of Political Faith* (1957), Shklar employs the distinction between the Enlightenment and the Counter-Enlightenment to trace "modern man's decline of confidence" in metaphysical certainty. I use the distinction to describe the decline of confidence in the institutions and practices of parliamentary democracy.

Both Shklar and Berlin describe the political philosophy of the Enlightenment as "liberal" and the philosophies of the Counter-Enlightenment as "romantic." In this book, "liberalism" refers to the ideas and the political prescriptions of Enlightenment figures like the seventeenth-century philosopher John Locke and his disciples in the centuries following – the Lockean liberals, the constitutionalists. It is classicism in political dress.

In 1992 I gave a talk to the Liberal Studies Program at Brock University entitled "Liberals and Romantics." William Mathie, founder and director of the program, argued that I was trying to incorporate too many diverse trends of thought into "the romantic." I thought at the time that he had a point, and indeed he did. But now, more than a decade later, I take heart from Berlin. Berlin argues that the romantic movement says "everything and its opposite." Romanticism is a "wild wood." Romantics can be progressive and reactionary, communal and individualistic, political and apolitical. And so we'll find it in Canadian history and politics. What makes these diverse trends "romantic"? It will be one of our tasks to find out. The 1992 talk, considerably revised, appears in this book as Chapter Two, "Beyond Right-Centre-Left."

Finally, I wish to thank Oona Eisenstadt, Barbara Carroll, Sarah Halsted, and Curtis Fahey for helpful criticism.

PART ONE
Liberals and Romantics

1

Prenez Garde!

Watch your step!

Imagine taking the train to work. The conductor sees you up the iron steps. You sidle along to a seat, stow your briefcase, and sit down. But you don't take your coat off. Like every one on the coach, you keep on your toque, scarf, coat, gloves, and boots. It's expected. You're familiar with the practice. There's nothing for it but to sweat out the journey. (The temperature on the train is a clement 25° Celsius.)

It's the same at work. A pleasant office, well equipped. You have interesting projects ahead. There's just the awkward requirement that in a well-heated room you must keep buttoned up. Coat, hat, scarf. But so it's been for years. You've sometimes thought of changing jobs. But it would mean moving to another country. This is Canada. Buttoned up is the rule, and it's the same everywhere in polite society. The coat bunches, pinches and drags. But you keep it on. It's your uniform. It defines you.

In this book I suggest that our perceptions of Canadian history and politics are like that bunchy, pinchy coat. They don't fit; they chafe and prevent free action; they're stifling us. Think of my argument as an invitation to disrobe. And what do I propose you slip into? Something old, something new, something borrowed, something blue?

The standard account of our history and political culture in political science textbooks says that British North America was – and Canada today still is – a more conservative nation than the

United States, more "tory" in a good old-fashioned sense. There's supposedly a streak of conservative deference in our make-up. We're less ruthlessly committed to equalitarianism. We're more law-abiding. Moreover – so goes the argument – we're more willing to sacrifice individual interests to the common good. The same toryism that encourages deference leads us to look on big government with a sceptically friendly eye.

It may sound paradoxical to attribute Canadian support for the welfare state and medicare to a conservative streak in our political culture. But that's the argument. Supposedly Canadians understand, as Americans do not, that a more orderly society requires public programs for the benefit of all, and specially programs for the benefit of the disadvantaged.

More caring. More orderly. Sounds good? Sounds Canadian? It's certainly true that many Canadians, perhaps the majority, see their nation in just this fashion. But it's also true that others don't see things this way. And here's where the overcoat bunches and pinches.

We've got a one-size national identity that doesn't fit all our citizens. Consider the matter of gun registration. It's probable that the majority of Canadians favour laws to compel registration of long guns. And in a liberal democracy the majority makes the decisions for all, through our representatives in the legislature. So on one level there's no problem. Most Canadians want gun laws, and all Canadians are going to get them. That's the way a democracy works. Everything's fair and square. Or is it?

Remember the standard description of the Canadian identity says that we're a people who favour law and order. We leave law and order to the professionals. We "naturally" shrink from carrying guns. It follows that true Canadians will favour gun control as a matter of course. It's in keeping with our identity. But think! What about those opposed? Are we supposed to regard them as less than fully Canadian? Shall we say that they don't quite measure up in the Canadian identity stakes? It's one thing to lose a debate in the legislative arena. It happens all the time. It's part of living in a liberal democracy – but it's another thing to have one's national identity called in question.

The quarrel over gun laws is a minor matter: a missing sleeve button, a few loose threads. One such issue doesn't make a major crisis. Yet there are other similar issues, some more serious, including almost all the policies connected with the welfare and regulatory state. Insofar as we believe that true, buttoned-up Canadians favour welfarism, we can't fully and freely debate all measures. Don't suppose that I'm arguing against the welfare state here. I'm not arguing against welfare measures, and I'm not arguing against gun registration. What I'm suggesting is that, in a liberal democracy, questions of national identity shouldn't limit public deliberation on policy. Free and open deliberation on measures for the common good is the hallmark of liberal democracy. We're in danger of forgetting that idea.

We've come to think that there are some subjects from which the loyal Canadian should avert her thoughts. There are some policy options she should not embrace. We laugh at the United States for its belief that certain attitudes and policies are un-American. We tell ourselves that we have no category labelled "un-Canadian." How wrong we are. I suggest in the following chapters that our buttoned-up identity hampers debate on multiculturalism, globalization, aboriginal identity, Quebec's distinctiveness, and constitutional reform.

The fact that our debates are constricted is a symptom of another problem. Canadians don't think in a large and generous way, in a philosophical way, about what it is to live in a liberal democracy. Of course, there are books on Canadian democracy. There are books on "Canadian political thought." And many of them are valuable. But most have a narrow focus and few sympathetically explore the principles of liberal democracy and parliamentary government. We live with the institutions of liberal democracy, but we barely know them. We have our set ways, our set ideas. We have familiar routines. We have familiar disagreements.

In this book I encourage you to step out of some old ideas and into some new ones. I argue especially that the time has come to examine our liberal-democratic constitution, not with a view to reforming it or discarding it but to see what is valuable, what has stood the test of time, what will endure. I am going to make the best case I can for Canada's once and future democracy.

THE CANADA WE NEVER WERE

Advocates of the more caring-and-peaceable definition of Canada argue that our identity is the product of our political and social history. Dame History herself gave it to us. She stitched it, she fitted it, and who are we to complain about bunchiness and loose threads?

It's said that our conservative streak originated with the United Empire Loyalists, the American Tories who remained true to the British crown at the time of the Revolution and proved it by leaving the republic for British North America. They're supposed to have been imbued with a willingness to defer to elites and to put the common good above individual interests and – so goes the argument – they stamped these notions on the political life of their new home. The colonial oligarchies (the Family Compact, the Chateau Clique) were tory in this sense. The Fathers of Confederation were tory.

But this account's wrong. Wrong from start to finish. The Loyalists weren't purveyors of a benign teaching about deference and collectivism. They didn't come to the British territories hoping to find a society where they could bow the knee and doff the cap. They were American liberals (or most of them were) imbued with ideas of liberal individualism. They had many reasons for leaving the United States, but the desire to live out their lives in docile subordination wasn't one of them. The first thing they did when they arrived in the western wilds of the old province of Quebec was to demand a representative legislative assembly. They argued that free political institutions were their right as British subjects.

And the men of the Family Compact and Chateau Clique did not put the common good above individual interest. They were oligarchs; they used their position in government to feather their individual nests at the expense of the common good. Nor were the Fathers of Confederation ideological tories in the standard definition. Some were Conservatives. Others were Liberals. But whether capital-c Conservative or capital-l Liberal, they weren't deferential, collectivist conservatives in the old-fashioned sense. They were liberal democrats. They designed a free constitution for a free country. In brief, the documentary evidence doesn't support the current textbook account of our history. And the idea of Canada that's drawn from it is equally suspect.

In *Canada's Origins* (1995), Peter J. Smith and I argued that recent Canadian historians and political scientists get our history wrong because they're trying to make facts and arguments fit a Marxian model, which describes a march of political ideologies from the seventeenth century to the present – first tory ideology, then liberalism, and then, in the late nineteenth century and in our own time, socialism. Conservatism, liberalism, socialism. Right, centre, left. Even scholars who believe themselves a world away from Hegel and Marx have come to rely on this notion of a necessary evolution of political ideas in modern history. It's the standard teaching in introductory textbooks in political science. And under its influence it becomes easy to suppose that British North America was once conservative according to the old tory definition, that the Dominion of Canada became more liberal in the years after Confederation, and that later still, at some point in the twentieth century, Canadians added a little socialism to the mix, just enough to give us our present welfare system.

Perhaps you're thinking that all this sounds familiar. We were once more conservative, became more liberal, and are now a liberal democracy tempered by socialism. Maybe the old overcoat isn't such a bad fit! And perhaps you're thinking as well that at least the story ends up in the right place, with the Canadian welfare state. Nothing wrong with that! (I might agree.)

So what am I complaining about? I suggested above that our restrictive definition of Canadian identity puts a crimp in public deliberation; it limits democracy. There's the same problem with the march of ideologies. Democrats like to think that laws and policies result from public demand and debate, but the march-of-ideologies model (right-centre-left) says that history nudges us in the direction of a particular agenda. We don't choose freely; at each new stage of our evolution we find ourselves favouring policies "appropriate" for the times. Willy nilly. There's no real debate. Some people have seen the future; they're right, and they'll win eventually. And those who try to argue for a different agenda just haven't caught on.

(There's worse: the idea that history's going "somewhere,"

that there is one ideological goal, one political pattern, to which we'll all adhere sooner or later, encourages one-party government, even one-party *tyranny*. But that's a subject for later.)

I'm not claiming to have made a sufficient argument against historical determinism. My point is merely that it's hard to reconcile such determinism with democracy in any ordinary definition.

THE TWO DEMOCRACIES

In the following chapters, I argue that Canadian history and Canadian politics still reveals today, not a necessary progression of ideologies from conservatism through liberalism to socialism, but an ongoing debate, a *back-and-forth*, between two (perhaps more, but certainly two) political visions, two political movements. Liberalism is one. The liberalism of John Locke, I contend, was present from earliest days in British North America and still shapes our institutions and culture. The other vision is ...

Well, what *is* the other one? That's the question. In *Canada's Origins* I accepted the idea that the other ideology is what Peter Smith calls "civic republicanism." Civic republicanism, as Smith defines it, is a philosophy of community. It has at its heart the Aristotelian idea of the virtuous and participatory citizenry. Thus, Smith and I saw the politics of Canada's nineteenth century as a contest (or, in heated moments, armed struggle) between individualists and "communitarians," that is, between Lockean liberals and civic republicans. Our approach brought to light a hitherto unnoticed debate about the nature of democracy.

By "unnoticed," I mean that no one had detected it in British North America. The debate itself is a great one and well known. It's been going on from the eighteenth century, and is still with us today. The simplest way to think of it is as a quarrel between those who want "strong" democracy, a form of government that encourages all to participate in the institutions of rule (or perhaps corrals and forces all), and those who want "liberal democracy," a form in which participation is freely allowed but remains voluntary and devotion to private life is valued as much.

I think it's surprising that no one had seen this debate on democracy in the pre-Confederation period, and I think Smith and I did well to uncover it. I like Smith's suggestion that civic republicanism is strongly present in our history. We said true things. And yet! I begin to think that the communal philosophy we turned up owes more to Rousseau than to Aristotle. It is modern in origin, not ancient. In addition, I now think that there was something going on in the colonies that our neat opposition between Lockean liberalism and civic republicanism didn't capture. Civic republicanism in bare description is a rather tidy, even prudish doctrine. Everyone toes the line in the republican community. All strive to be virtuous according to the same definition of virtue. I still believe that civic republicanism was present in the colonies. But I have come to think it sometimes allied itself to a political passion that is anything but prudish. There's a wild side to political thought in British North America. There's something enticingly unpredictable. Something modern and dangerous.

I call that enticing, dangerous ideology "romanticism." Romanticism easily embraces ideas of strong democracy but also yearns for individual freedom and self-fulfilment. It's a paradoxical ideology; indeed, it's not an ideology proper, but rather it's a mode of thought, a "movement," a perspective that informs politics, art, religion, and philosophy from some time towards the end of the eighteenth century. "The importance of romanticism," says Isaiah Berlin, "is that it is the largest recent movement to transform the lives and the thought of the Western world." He adds: "It seems to me to be the greatest single shift in the consciousness of the West that has occurred, and all the other shifts that have occurred in the course of the nineteenth and twentieth centuries appear to me less important, and at any rate deeply influenced by it."

Following Berlin, I argue that the politics of the modern period pits Enlightenment liberalism against Counter-Enlightenment romanticism. The debate about the nature of democracy is best understood in this context. We'll see the once and future Canadian democracy in proper perspective when we stop trying to sort events and ideas into categories of right, centre, and left (when we shed our bunchy overcoats) and ask instead whether our history and our politics today is informed by an opposition between liberalism and romanticism.

2

Beyond Right-Centre-Left

Political scientists typically locate political ideologies and programs – ideas about the way political things ought to go – on a continuum from "right" to "left." We speak of three Canadian ideologies: conservatism, liberalism and socialism. Right, centre, left. Or we used to.

In the last chapter, I argued that students of political culture define conservatism as the ideology of deference and collectivism, and liberalism as the ideology of equality and liberty. Socialism supposedly brings the two together: it's the synthesis, marrying collectivism and equality. These definitions are alive and well in public discourse. Think of the term "red tory." Canadians use it to argue that some conservatives are sympathetic to the collectivist objectives of socialists. And indeed, as I've suggested, some believe that red toryism – a dignified concern for the disadvantaged – virtually defines Canada.

But words slip around. In day-to-day debates, Canadians also use "conservative" and "tory" to describe someone who's stingy with money, more likely to favour the rich than the poor. Especially when we're thinking of the government's use of public money (who gets "what, when, and how"), we say that the conservative is someone who thinks governments should tax less, spend less, and leave people alone as much as possible to get on with their private lives. In the same mode, we say that liberals believe governments should spend more and regulate the economy, reign in the business interests, and assist the disadvantaged.

Everyone admits the ideological labels don't fit the political parties very well. In the typical introductory politics class, students are taught that the Liberal Party of Canada includes members who resemble conservatives because they are sympathetic to business and wary of public enterprise, but also "welfare liberals" who can barely be distinguished from socialists. They're also told that capital-c Conservatives who hope to "roll back big government" are really liberals, "liberal" as the term was used in the eighteenth and nineteenth centuries.

Confusing? In my opinion it's not so important that the definitions of "conservatism" and "liberalism" slide around and that "right," "centre," and "left" don't describe the parties. What's important, however, is that these labels don't describe Canadian politics.

Right-centre-left (r-c-l) was never adequate and today its deficiencies are more obvious than ever. We don't learn from a person's position on the right-centre-left continuum where he or she stands on a host of issues that are at least as important to Canadians as "who gets what." Especially we don't learn where she or he stands on the issue of democracy and political participation.

What first alerted me to r-c-l's deficiencies was the Spicer Report of 1991. Asked to find out what the Canadian grassroots was thinking about constitutional reform, the Spicer Commission uncovered a rising tide of political discontent. It seemed, at least from this one survey, that Canadians didn't like very much about the Canadian political system, and liked even less the various proposals the federal and provincial governments were putting forward to reform it. Where on r-c-l, I wondered, does one locate that kind of dissatisfaction? Note that what the commission turned up was not merely dissatisfaction with particular programs and policies. Grumbling about particular policies is par for the course in a liberal democracy. It's expected and – supposedly – welcome. It's the inevitable consequence of free speech in a free country. What the commission revealed was dissatisfaction on a deeper level, dissatisfaction with the very system that produces policies, with parliamentary liberal democracy, with partisan politics and opportunities for political participation. Canadians seemed to be saying that liberal democracy isn't good enough and, especially, not democratic enough.

The demand for more democracy is associated with the Canadian Reform and Alliance parties (said to be on the right because sympathetic to business and the market) but also with groups like the National Action Committee on the Status of Women, considered "left" because they favour the expansion of government programs and regulations. In the past, direct democracy was urged by the Progressive Party and by the Cooperative Commonwealth Federation (the CCF, Canada's founding socialist party).

We need a new model. Out with r-c-l, conservative, liberal, and socialist! I propose that we adopt the terms "romantic" and "liberal." The two Canadian political ideologies are romanticism and liberalism. No particular set of programs can be unambiguously identified with these ideologies. (Especially, there is no blue book, or red book, for romanticism.) Neither is concerned above all with money – who gets what and when. It may be that some liberals have more respect for the accumulation of material goods than some romantics; it may be that some romantics incline to socialism. But so do some liberals, as I've noted. When all's said and done, neither liberalism nor romanticism takes its stand on getting and spending. Both set their goals higher. Romantics dream of democracy as individual self-fulfilment and the expression of communal identity. Liberals cherish freedom and justice.

No, we are not going to find it easy to draw up tidy programs labelled "liberal" and "romantic." Nevertheless, I believe that the liberal-romantic distinction has substance.

NEW POLITICS

Political scientists sometimes use the term "new politics" or "post-materialist politics" to describe the aims of political individuals and groups that can't be subsumed under the conservative, liberal, and socialist labels. New politics, it's said, is characterized by lack of confidence in the system, distrust of politicians, dissatisfaction with opportunities for effective citizen-participation, and impatience with political forms and formalities. It's concerned with opening opportunities for expression of political demands, and with "recognition" of marginalized groups. In brief, it's about participation and group identity rather than with "who gets what."

"New politics" suggests that what is being described is an unprecedented phenomenon. Some political scientists describe it as a function of "post-industrialism." But in my opinion the so-called new politics is merely a recent form of romanticism, a trend of thought with deep roots in history. In Canada it's as old as Louis-Joseph Papineau, leader of the Rebellions of 1837–38. And in the Western nations generally, it's as old as the eighteenth-century philosopher Jean Jacques Rousseau.

I might have chosen populism, simple democracy, or even communitarianism to describe this romantic, new-politics ideology. All these terms have some thing to recommend them. They all describe aspects of the one underlying attitude. I prefer "romantic." It suggests enthusiasm, yearning – impatience. In my view, impatience is central to the romantic ideology, whatever the particular form, whatever the era.

From the old r-c-l scheme we have to rescue the term "liberal," by which I mean the liberalism of the seventeenth-century philosopher John Locke. Liberalism, properly understood, signifies much more than middle-of-the road indecisiveness about the welfare state and government interventionism. It is indeed an ideology of liberty. It was born of resistance to the political absolutism of seventeenth-century Europe, and at its heart is the idea – so splendid in the opinion of liberals, so chilling when perceived by romantics – that law can make you free.

I've argued that r-c-l is deficient because it doesn't capture the full range of our thinking about how things ought to go in politics. Another reason for rejecting it is that it invites one to think in terms of historical progression. It portrays conservatives as reluctant liberals, men and women unable to free themselves from the stale ideas of the past. It portrays liberals as "wannabe" socialists, afraid to take the leap. It argues, indeed, that socialism lies ahead in the modern world as surely as the seasons turn.

But the idea of a necessary progression towards socialism came tumbling down with the Berlin Wall. Let me suggest that, rather than taking liberalism as a stage on the way to something else, we see it as one of the enduring modern political alternatives. The great alternatives in the politics of the modern era have been and are today Enlightenment liberalism and Counter-Enlightenment romanticism.

THE ROMANTIC

In Canada's National Election Survey (NES), a poll routinely put to a careful sample of Canadians in election years, political scientists ask a number of questions to elicit citizens' attitudes to democracy and participation. Here's one question, said to elicit the dimension of our political culture called "political efficacy." It's useful for us because it speaks to the deep heart of romanticism: "Does anyone in power listen to you?"

No! says the romantic. No one in power listens to me.

I won't deny that it's easy to conclude no one listens. Given our multi-party system and first-past-the-post elections, I'm likely to end up voting for a losing candidate. And even if my candidate wins, his or her party may not emphasize the political measures that are closest to my heart. My favourite projects may be dropped from the party program, or from the legislative schedule. I don't get what I want.

Many people understand that elections are a poor means of conveying policy instructions to government. What the romantic perspective adds is profound dissatisfaction with this state of affairs. For the romantic, it's appalling that the most common and most honoured form of interaction between rulers and ruled – the electoral process – offers voters so little scope. Elections ought to empower the voters.

Schemes for reform proliferate in this area, all with a romantic following. Does the problem lie with our party system? If we got rid of our old-line, middle-of-the-road parties that try to be all things to as many people as possible, if we introduced new parties with clearly differentiated programs – "programmatic parties" – would things improve? We'd have to change the electoral system to get such parties. And why not? say the romantics. If our so-called representative assemblies at the federal and provincial levels more closely mirrored Canadians' opinions, wouldn't things improve? We could go a long way in this direction. We could devise assemblies to provide an exact reflection of class, gender, and ethnicity in the electorate! We could adopt statistical representation, in which pollsters selected our representatives. What the heck, we could abolish assemblies, send the representatives home and rely on polls.

Some point the finger at the parliamentary form of government because, they say, it allows leaders of the party securing the most seats in the House Commons to govern virtually unchecked between elections. We have "cabinet oligarchy," it's said, not democracy. Would changing the electoral system help?

Making party organizations more democratic, enhancing constituency control of elected representatives through such devices as referendums, the initiative, and the recall, strengthening local governments, decentralizing, devolving decision making to localities – these are remedies that appeal to the romantic. Governing from the grassroots.

Liberals, too, are interested in some of these reforms. They aren't entirely averse to reform. The term "progress" sometimes falls from the liberal's lips. Most liberals would agree that we need a more effective opposition in the Canadian Parliament and in the provincial legislatures. But, beside the romantics, liberals are sticks-in-the-mud, much less convinced that the system has to be changed, and not at all convinced that it has to be changed holus-bolus.

Romantics insist, they demand, they want. They may even contemplate rebellion. Though romantics talk about the value of community and the shared life, when push comes to shove, some of them are ready to fling off the constraints of our shared life in liberal democracy and take to the streets. Throwing rocks at Starbucks and McDonald's supposedly gives the marginalized a "voice" denied by liberal democracy. It expresses disdain for materialism and the selfishness of liberal capitalism.

In the streets, in Parliament, in the classroom, in the boardroom (!), the romantic yearns to liberate us from our shackles. The decent, hidebound, decorous, bourgeois, notions of freedom embraced by liberalism are stifling. Here's romanticism at its wildest. Preaching a doctrine of extreme liberty.

And yet romantics shrink from the adversarial politics of the parliamentary system. They endorse confrontation but heap scorn on the decorous contestation of parties, leaders, and lobbies in today's politics. They are easily fired by dreams of collectivity. Ask what you can do for your country! At the heart of the romantic vision – as some see it – is the hope that Canadians will discover consensus.

In the debates of the early 1990s on constitutional reform, it was commonly said that the parliamentary process is inherently unsatisfactory because "adversarial and majoritarian." What's needed, said one theorist, is "a process that not only hears all voices but takes all experiences and aspirations into account." In their hearts, romantics want more than electoral and parliamentary change. They want a politics and society in which all say "yes" with one strong voice. There *is* a way to reconcile individual self-realization and community. There must be!

THE LIBERAL

In defining liberal ideology, we could do worse than turn again to the NES. There, we found romanticism by asking a question that elicits attitudes to "political efficacy." For liberalism, we can use the questions that measure the dimension called "political trust."

I don't want to suggest that liberals are by nature trusting. Not at all. The liberal boasts about her political scepticism. "Eternal vigilance is the price of liberty." Liberals don't trust leaders; they don't trust anyone who exercises political power. "All power corrupts and absolute power corrupts absolutely." On occasion they, too – like the romantics – have resorted to rebellion, though most of the liberal rebellions are far in the past. Their first rebellion, and perhaps their greatest, was the Glorious Revolution of 1688 in Britain, which disposed once and for all of the divine right of kings and established Parliament on the basis of popular sovereignty. Their most famous was the American Revolution.

In short, liberals know how *not* to trust. It remains that they are far more inclined than romantics to think that a degree of trust in political institutions (not in politicians, but in institutions) is commendable. And they are inclined to express confidence – a suitably dubious confidence, in the institutions of their own polity. They reserve the highest degree of trust for the principles underlying the liberal-democratic constitution: "the rule of law," the principle of representative democracy, individual and political freedoms, toleration of dissent, and so on. Thus, a question on "political trust" may reveal the liberal. I suggest this one: What should citizens expect from government?

What should the citizen expect from government? The answer springs from the liberal's heart: "The right to life, liberty and the pursuit of happiness." "Peace, Order and Good Government."

The liberal believes that these objectives are best realized in a regime that encourages adversarial politics and honours dissent, features of liberal democracy sometimes deplored by romantics, as I have said. According to the liberal, it's just a fact of political life that people disagree on fundamental issues, including, of course, "who gets what." Dissidents will never vanish from the face of the earth. The romantic dream of consensus is just so much baloney.

The party system in liberal democracies enables and constrains this divisiveness. Because a party holding office can never claim to represent all the people, because it can never claim to speak for the whole community – it is, after a "part" of the system, a "party" – its laws and pronouncements are always open to challenge, and its leaders can legitimately be turned out of office. Therein lies our freedom, says the liberal.

Liberals laugh at the romantic hankering for effective elections. Elections don't convey a policy mandate to leaders. (There are other ways to do that.) The supreme benefit of elections is they enable us to get parties and leaders out of office. In the liberal's view, parties naturally want to remain in power forever. Parties and leaders are endlessly ambitious. It's our job as citizens to know when and how to thwart them.

We imagine the liberal saying, it's so like romantics to want to tear up the system – or tear it down – when the problem really is that they don't understand how it works. The slightest hint that they're not getting their way and the romantic girds himself for the barricades. Or he sulks. That's the liberal view of romanticism.

I said that the liberal is prepared to think about reforms – not the grand schemes that the romantic cherishes. Moderate reforms. In the area of participatory politics, the liberal may want more measures to protect dissent and free speech. She is likely to want more checks and balances, more respect for political opposition – in short, a system that is *more* adversarial.

Romantics may think of improving the system to make it more efficient ("political efficacy"), but the liberal dreams of slowing things up. "Sober second thought." Liberals put great store in the fact that free governments can repeal measures.

But perhaps I've gone too far. There are liberals and liberals. Of course. The liberal camp cherishes diversity! There are liberals more enamoured of efficiency and liberals less enamoured.

Yet one thing all true liberals agree on – more or less – is that attempts to reform human nature are suspect. A longing for community and consensus sometimes drives the romantic to think about encouraging political virtue in public life. A virtuous citizenry, political leaders of stainless merit – that's the dream of some romantics. Dream away, says the liberal. No doubt there are good men and women. No doubt some selfless men and women will be moved to seek public office. But it's far more likely that public office will attract individuals anxious above all to further their own ambition and careers. Politics attracts bullies. What liberal-democratic institutions offer, according to liberals, is the means to harness selfishness and ambition and force them into channels that will serve the public good. Constrained by good institutions, the untrustworthy find themselves pursuing measures that the trustworthy would endorse.

There you have it: liberalism and romanticism. In my view, this scheme explains a great deal more about what's going on in Canada and in the world than the old continuum model, r-c-l, conservative, liberal, socialist. True, it doesn't describe Canadian political parties. Liberalism-romanticism doesn't offer much of an improvement on r-c-l in this respect. But it does describe our deep hearts. It does describe Canadian politics.

So out with r-c-l, right-centre-left? I think so. We may still find the terms "right" and "left" useful to describe attitudes on government taxing and spending. We'll probably still call prudent liberals "conservative." Some romantics and liberals will go on calling themselves socialists. There's no reason to get rid of all the old terms, and every reason to keep them. But the idea of a historical progression has to be discarded. Right-centre-left doesn't *explain*.

Political scientists have been entrapped by the r-c-l model for decades now. When it's time to introduce the first-year class to political ideology, right-centre-left dominates the agenda. "Conservatism harks back to the eighteenth century and before," the professor reads from his notes. "Liberalism emerges from the struggle against conservatism in the early modern period, and socialism, in its turn, derives from the failure of liberalism to account for man's natural desire for community." That's how the lecture goes, or used to go, and while there is a little bit of truth in it, consider that it offers only a caricature of liberalism. Liberal democracy becomes that way station on history's ruthless march to the future, a brief stop on the royal road to socialism. The constitutional dimension of liberal democracy (the rule of law, individual and political freedom, representative institutions, responsible and accountable government, toleration of free political speech) is barely mentioned, except to note the inevitability of its demise.

And what about romanticism – the ideology that is taking the professor's students into the streets, firing them with the sentiments of anti-globalism, stoking their hunger for a world in which their are no injustices, no inequalities, teaching them to fling off the constraints of law, teaching them to rely on virtue – their own virtuous vision of a better world? About romanticism, r-c-l says nothing!

The professor is silent about romanticism. It's alive and well in the auditorium before him. But he's reading from old notes.

3

The Evil Futures

The vision of consensus, the idea that all citizens will say "yes" with one strong voice – this is romanticism at its craziest, says the liberal. It's *hopelessly* romantic.

LIBERALS ON THE SUMMUM MALUM

Romantic, yes. But is it "hopeless"? A deep stratum of liberal thought believes the romantic vision of consensus is only too feasible, and very dangerous. The romantic longing for consensus puts us on the slippery slope to the Nazi Holocaust, the Soviet Gulags, the killing fields of Cambodia, the deliberate starvation of millions in the Ukraine under Stalin, the "ethnic cleansings" of the Balkans, and the horrendous death tolls, perhaps more than forty million, in the People's Republic of China. Utopianism that leads to the killing fields: this is liberalism's idea of the *summum malum*. The greatest political evil.

We have barely begun to come to terms with the fact that the twentieth century was one of the bloodiest in history. We know the numbers: six million died, ten million, forty million. But we let our attention slip away. There is a natural human propensity to turn one's thoughts from deeply unpleasant and deeply frightening facts. It is not the worst thing about us that we would rather think about proposals for peace, collective action to help refugees, ways to improve world health, and so on. We subsume the great killings of the twentieth century under more familiar headings. After all, we tell ourselves, death on a grand scale has always been a feature of human history. People die in war, from disease, famine, natural disasters. Thus, we avert our thoughts from the truly extraordinary thing about the last century, which is that people died in unprecedented numbers as a result of deliberate action by the state of which they were citizens or subjects. Great numbers were *murdered*. It is true that states have often been careless about human lives. They execute some individuals; they allow others to die of neglect. The twentieth century was different because the campaigns involved so many, were carried out over long periods with great energy, and were justified by elaborate ideological posturing.

Liberals sometimes profess to see a romanticism of the "right" and a romanticism of the "left." They put the Nazi murders in one category ("right wing") and the Soviet murders in another ("left wing"). I would never argue that the particular histories of the massacres are unimportant. Generalizations about such things blunt the sensibilities. But there is one striking feature that the state-sponsored killings of the twentieth century have in common. Whether fascist, communist, or nationalist, the perpetrators spoke the language of absolute democracy – or, as the liberals say – *romantic* democracy. The killings were done in the name of "the people" or "the nation."

In mild form, romantic democracy appears to be nothing more than a crude majoritarianism in which those who claim to be the "people" – usually the poor – lord it over the minority – usually the wealthy. But that's only the beginning, says the liberal. Soon the poor themselves are groaning under the yoke of their professed representatives. Political leaders emerge who claim sole authority to represent the class of the poor, or the way of life that is the nation, or the republican virtue to which all should aspire. Dissent then appears like opposition to the general will, opposition to virtue, opposition to a happy future. And so are forged the chains of absolute democracy.

All struggle to exhibit the required opinions, virtue, character. Citizens form herds, they flock like animals, calling themselves, free, virtuous, and happy. And then begin the programs to eliminate recalcitrant "animals," those who won't or can't conform. Here we must imagine the romantic breaking in, outraged at the idea that romanticism leads to totalitarianism. How can you suppose there's any connection between romanticism, which honours the creative freedom of the individual, and the dreary regimentation and suppression that characterizes totalitarian regimes? Think of the goose-stepping parades passing Hitler's viewing stand, the chants of praise all shouted at the top of the voice in unison to a dreary beat. Think of the public tributes to Stalin, more endless masses again, all in step, all shouting the same thing, all supposedly *thinking* the same thing. No romantic could have designed those dreadful displays. No romantic participated. Totalitarianism is the antithesis of romanticism. Think of how the artists suffered in those days. The least hint of individuality was a virtual death sentence.

But the liberal is not convinced. Romanticism's attack on liberal prudence, its ruthless insistence on the life of integrity, may indeed support intolerant forms of rule. Romanticism swings between wild individualism, which leaves no room for the kind of government that imposes the laws liberals believe necessary for freedom, and wild enthusiasm for total participation in nationalist forms of cultural life.

Does romanticism lead to totalitarianism? What do the scholars say? Judith Shklar argues that extreme forms of political nationalism were not originally part of romantic thought but represent its degeneracy. "That romanticism was eventually put to the service of ... politics was the last of the many self-inflicted defeats of romanticism." Isaiah Berlin appears to agree. "Fascism ... is an inheritor of romanticism," he argues. "The hysterical self-assertion and the nihilistic destruction of existing institutions because they confine the unlimited will, which is the only thing that counts for human beings; the superior person who crushes the inferior because his will is stronger; these [characteristics of fascism] are a direct inheritance – in an extremely distorted and garbled form, no doubt, but still an inheritance – from the romantic movement."

Did liberalism's earliest thinkers understand romanticism? Did they see dangers coming? So I would argue. In what I've said to this point, I've followed Berlin in dating romanticism from the end of the eighteenth century. It's certainly at the end of the eighteenth century that some poets and philosophers, the ones we commonly call "romantic," came to see themselves as a movement in opposition to the European Enlightenment. But there's an older quarrel that's relevant. We might describe it as the opposition between prophecy and prudence and it's as old as the Bible. The Biblical prophets demand adherence to moral absolutes and formulate their prescriptions in light of the end of politics and the end of history. The Biblical priests are more pragmatic; they devise a "doable" program for a people living in this world of ambiguities. This is not the place to tell the whole story of the tension between prophecy and prudence. It's a feature of the Greek tradition as well as the Biblical. Nor is this the place to explore differences between ancient and modern extremism. What we can say is that John Locke, writing in the seventeenth century, understands well the dangers in political enthusiasm generated by the competition of religious enthusiasts for public status.

Locke falls out on the side of the "priests." He is a realist. His remedy differs in all details from that of the Biblical priests but it has a similar objective. It is meant to reign in religious intransigence and religious enthusiasm while still allowing, indeed encouraging, religious belief. What Locke recommended we now accept as the coping stone of modern liberal democracies: the separation of church and state. Affiliation with a particular religious denomination would no longer confer an absolute right to govern. Indeed, Locke argues more generally that birth, family, ethnic, and tribal associations should offer no political advantage. His prescription is now so familiar that it's easy to forget how truly novel it was. What he proposed in brief was to remove from the realm of politics and public administration all of humanity's dearest objectives, everything closest to the human heart: love of God, love of family, pride in one's particularity. He proposed in short to take the romance out of politics.

Politics would become an altogether a tamer affair. Political leaders would no longer compete in the public realm for life's greatest prizes. It would be their job rather to serve the people and to secure life and liberty, peace, order, and good government, so that each citizen can pursue happiness as she or he defines it. Locke's argument, in brief, is that liberal democracy, well maintained, with due vigilance and care, prevents the *summum malum*.

There are remedies, says the liberal. There are rational solutions to political ills. Don't despair. At the heart of liberalism lies an incorrigible optimism.

THE ROMANTIC'S SUMMUM MALUM

The romantic's *summum malum* resembles the liberal's in bare outline. Ignorant armies clash by night. Great masses of people are enslaved. But the romantic doesn't blame these evils on an excess of utopianism. Oh no! It's not an excess of moral enthusiasm that is threatening to destroy us. It's too little morality and too little enthusiasm. And in the minds of many romantics the tidy remedies proposed by liberals – like separation of church and state – are part of the problem.

Here we encounter a difficulty. I have been speaking of liberalism and romanticism as if they were comparable phenomena. They are not. Liberalism is a political doctrine. It requires conformity to the principles of toleration and respect for minorities in public life, but supposedly those very principles allow and indeed encourage heterodoxy in the private realm. Locke inveighed against the political ambitions of religious leaders, not against religion. He banished nepotism, not family affection. Thus, liberals embrace romantic music, art, and philosophy – in the home, in the universities, in the concert hall. Romantic music – of course, of course! It is the greatest the world has known. Romantic novels? Who can resist? The romantic poets and philosophers? Blake, Byron, Coleridge, Herder, Heidegger, Hoelderlin, Rousseau, Schiller, Schelling, Schliermacher, Splenger, the poets of the *Sturm und Drang*. Of course. Every educated man and woman reads them. Or reads about them. That's the liberal argument. It's tolerant, decent, intellectually curious.

Romanticism, in contrast, is only sometimes political. As I have suggested, it is a teaching, or an attitude, that calls for integrity of self and integrity in one's course of life. "Purity of heart is to will one thing." Thus, for romantics, the public-private, politics-society distinction is indefensible. It is patronizing. Romanticism isn't something you dip into in your off-hours. It can't be picked up and laid down. It certainly can't be appropriated in a one-term course entitled Western Civilization. What man or woman who has experienced the greatest works of human genius, who understands the glory and despair of the human situation as Art reveals it, can then go out to debate decorous political measures under Robert's Rules of Order? Only the domesticated, shrunken soul of the liberal would suppose it possible. Romanticism must be lived! It must be one's life. And so on.

From the romantic's perspective, the liberal's attempt to enjoy romantic works and teachings reduces them to dust and ashes. The True, the Beautiful, the Good isn't captured in tidy files, descriptions, and abstractions. Liberals do not understand beauty; they do not understand the unique. All their experiences are flat and shallow. They are essentially bourgeois, of the masses, "souls without longing." Even their descriptions of ugliness and evil are inescapably prosaic.

Thus, while romantics fear totalitarianism as much as liberals do, they describe it differently. The liberals' prosaic world will dominate. We will all be subjected to a wasteland of conformity in which people drag themselves through existence, never knowing life. Materialism dominates. The spirit is defeated. Some philosophers call this dreary future "the universal and homogeneous state." Today's romantic rebels call it "McWorld." All particular forms of identity, all religions, all national loyalties are submerged. Locke banished the sources of identity from public life and they continue today only in the shadows, in museums, in dusty archives, as objects of study in the wearisome institutions we call "universities." Proud cultures, ancient languages, high traditions are lost and people now spend their days and nights in pursuit of the unsatisfying pleasures required by capitalism.

In this picture the United States today appears not as the second home of liberal democracy but as the source of the universal consumerism that is destroying everything of moral and cultural worth in countries everywhere. It's the "restaurant at the end of the universe."

Pessimism comes easily to the romantic. If dreary totalitarianism is not our future, says the romantic, we will surely be engulfed by civil wars – another product of liberalism's essential pettiness. The classes, factions, special interests and individuals struggling for advantage within states have been urged on by the endless liberal chatter about individual gratification and the endless appeals to acquire, amass, and hoard. Society is splintering and falling apart. "The centre cannot hold."

The decline may begin as the wealthy withdraw to the suburbs and gated communities. Public schools and other communal endeavours fail. International cabals of the wealthy arise to exploit the poor on a larger scale. Imperialism was such a scheme, says the romantic. Patriarchy was such a scheme. So was racism, classism, empire: the campaigns to exploit the disadvantaged have many names. All of them originate in liberalism. Or so romantics argue.

The few flourish at the expense of the many. But in the competition for scarce goods the wealthy few are bound to fight among themselves. And then begins the complete decline of society in which liberalism's last pretence to justice and equality is overturned and cruel anarchy reigns, with its succession of quarrelling, petty tyrants and warlords.

The liberal professes to believe that these petty tyrants are armed with crazy notions of moral purpose, tribal loyalty, or religious enthusiasm. Think again, says the romantic. It's greed and self-aggrandizement that drives them, though they may justify their vicious acts with trumped-up arguments of one sort or another. And perhaps the worst of the situation is that ordinary decent people get caught up in these storms in ways that strip them of their last moral reserves. To defend their lives and families they put themselves under the uncertain protection of one faction and they then become a warlord's "muscle," doing evil to others.

Beware liberal greed, liberal blindness to the common good, liberal suspicion of "utopianism," says the romantic. Beware the vaunted liberal defence of dissent and opposition. Beware especially the selfishness of liberal capitalism!

ORIGINS

I said that liberalism was born in the seventeenth- and eighteenth-century struggle against Europe's absolute rulers. Yet it's not wrong to trace liberal arguments for the rule of law, human equality, and natural right to a much earlier period. It's not wrong to see a Biblical origin. The Bible says that all humanity is the offspring of one couple. There could hardly be a stronger assertion of human equality. There are no naturally superior peoples, no natural ruling races. We're all brothers and sisters originally. It's an idea profoundly congenial to both liberals and romantics, and it has never been forgotten in the prayers and hopes of the three great monotheistic religions, though often neglected and scorned in practice.

Nevertheless, in practical terms, modern liberalism emerges in the struggle against the Stuarts and the Bourbons. If liberal democracy celebrates a single birthday, it's 1688, the date of Britain's Glorious Revolution when the representatives of the people gained unquestioned ascendancy over the English kings and queens. For understandable reasons, Americans celebrate not 1688 but 1776. In the years before 1776, Americans had no difficulty acknowledging the liberalism of English government. They modelled their colonial governments on the British pattern and claimed for themselves the rights of Englishmen. But increasingly many came to believe that England was denying the American colonists those English rights. The British government was taking on autocratic powers resembling the powers of the hated Stuarts. Not all Americans adopted this opinion, as every Canadian learns (or used to learn) in Canadian history classes. Those who believed that connection with the British Empire offered a surer guarantee of individual and political rights came north to the colonies of British North America. Thus, in the documents and political debates of British North America and the Dominion of Canada, liberalism's birth date remains, as it is still in the British tradition of law, 1688.

For romantics, the efforts of 1688 were merely the promising beginning: "well begun, half done." The French Revolution followed. And the Russian. In the eyes of many romantics, these revolutions were the necessary continuation of the first. Some speak of the "world revolution" that began, perhaps, with 1688 but is still incomplete.

EVIL PASTS

Evil Futures, evil pasts. Locke rejected absolutism in all forms: monarchic, aristocratic, and democratic. But early in its history liberalism came to fear democratic absolutism above all.

Supposedly, liberalism welcomes parties, programs, and arguments of all political opinion. That's the theory, at any rate. No one is to be excluded. Oligarchs, aristocrats, democrats, let them all compete! The suggestion is that the extreme greed of oligarchs, the insufferable claims of aristocrats, and the jumped-up pretensions of the absolute democrats will be worn away in the give and take of political deliberation. The liberal constitution tempers extreme demands.

But in 1688 the kings and aristocrats went down to defeat, and today appeals to kingliness, caste, and inherited wealth count for little in political debate. What remains is the appeal to the *demos*. Locke taught that regimes must be grounded on popular consent, and this idea of popular consent, or "popular sovereignty," now underpins all modern polities. The difficulty is that this still-potent justification can claim for itself legitimacy not available to monarchists and aristocrats. All modern tyrannies describe their rule as the necessary working out of the democratic principle. Hence the liberal fear of democratic tyranny. History's democratic despots are the liberal bogey-men: Cromwell and Robespierre; in British North America, Louis-Joseph Papineau and William Lyon Mackenzie; and in our own time, Hitler, Stalin, Mao, Pol Pot.

And the romantics? I've said that romantics have an ambiguous attitude to politics. Many indeed are profoundly apolitical. But great political occasions, great revolutions, stir them to action. In the past they feared a return to the reign of the absolute monarchs. The Stuarts and Bourbons. At the time of the Canadian Rebellions in 1837-38, romantic rebels called for the exclusion of "sinister interests," and by sinister interests they meant the colonial elites and the imperialists.

Today they fear empire and oligarchy in new form, the "military-industrial complex" and the international cabal of moneyed interests. They contend that the cruelest regimes are those erected on the power that attaches to wealth. What nonsense to suppose that popular consent informs our present systems of rule. How blind liberals are! To counter oligarchy, the old prescription is the best: all efforts much be directed to establishing the power of the *demos*.

In short, liberals fear above all the tyranny of the "many" (or to be precise, the tyranny of individuals and parties that claim exclusive right to speak for the many), and they seek to erect against this danger an inclusive form of government with "checks and balances." Romantics fear the tyranny of "the few," rule by those who claim to be best but inevitably seek only their own interests, the moneyed crowd, the privileged, and to fend off tyranny in this form they go a long way towards demanding exclusive "power to the people." That's the form of the debate on democracy for much of the nineteenth century and it still is today. Liberals want liberal democracy; romantics want strong democracy.

PART TWO
Getting to Democracy

4

What Romantics Say

According to the liberals, something resembling democracy began in Britain in 1688. The people's representatives in Parliament had executed one king, fired another, and hired a third. The era of divine right was over. The era of popular sovereignty had begun. But few romantics date democracy from 1688. Indeed, many don't accept the idea that it arrived in British North America in 1867.

ARE WE THERE YET?
WHAT THE ROMANTICS SAY

Are we there yet? Romantics sometimes seem to be saying that democracy – true democracy – is forever beyond our reach. Romantics aren't tied to the idea that political ideologies and regimes unfold in a necessary sequence. They don't subscribe to models like "right-centre-left." Democracy happens. Or not.

Some observers professed to see a pleasant episode of democracy in street protests against the Ontario government organized by the Ontario Coalition Against Poverty in October 2001. Perhaps as many as 2,000 young people in balaclavas, scarves, and gas masks assembled in Toronto's business district. Armed with weapons familiar from demonstrations at Seattle and Quebec City, they made a show of confronting the police, threw rocks through windows, and rolled benches and mailboxes into the traffic. Some defecated on the sidewalks. They chanted "Our streets, our streets" and "This is what democracy looks like."

But after a few hours, "democracy" was over. The authorities detained about forty persons, out-of-town demonstrators climbed back on their bus, and the rush-hour traffic picked up.

In the romantics' reading of history, democracy surfaces in such moments and perhaps only in such moments. When the barricades go up and students stream out of classes, democracy arrives – for a while. When the army throws down its rifles and joins the students, when old institutions are overturned, when the walls come down: these are the democratic moments.

But after the demonstration, police restore the old order. And after a revolution the politicians gather to make a new constitution. Then the wretched process of institutional reconstruction begins, accompanied by begging, haggling, and compromise. The oligarchs slip back in and the people's voice dims.

Robert Frost wrote: "Nothing gold can stay." Many romantics believe that nothing democratic stays. But some do. From time to time, romantics involve themselves in schemes to make democracy "stay." We might call such romantics "divided souls." They hope to see democracy enshrined in bills of rights and constitutional clauses, but they also have to fight against the deep-seated romantic tendency to distrust constitutions and especially the process of making them.

In the first years of the French Revolution, many in England and some in North America thought that true, permanent democracy had arrived. The golden era! The institutions of the *ancien régime* were swept away and the pure, uncontested will of the people was about to shine forth. Romantic hearts beat high. But the democracy that ensued proved terrible indeed. As Wordsworth wrote, "Dark and more dark the shades of evening fell." Soon France and England were at war and in England programs for democratic reform (like the extension of the franchise and the elimination of the "rotten" electoral boroughs) lost appeal. "Democracy" became a bad word.

The same effect was felt in British North America. In 1810 Pierre Bédard, leader of the majority party in the Legislative Assembly of Lower Canada, went to jail for recommending – merely recommending – a change in the provincial constitution to bring it into line with British practice of the day. Bédard was no romantic; he was a liberal to the core, well read in English constitutional theory, an avid admirer of all things British in the realm of constitutional law. But in the chilly years after the Terror, anyone proposing constitutional reform was vulnerable. The stultifying colonial oligarchies were enjoying their heyday: the Family Compact, the Chateau Clique, the Maritime "official" parties.

By the 1830s, when the terms "reform" and "democracy" were once again allowed in polite intercourse, an intense debate started up among colonial romantics. The majority of them were determined to introduce at last constitutional reforms that would make democracy "stay."

In their newspapers, in pamphlets, and in formal manifestos, William Lyon Mackenzie and Louis-Joseph Papineau and their followers compiled ambitious programs of reform to devolve power to the people in perpetuity. Reform of the colonial legislative councils was a favourite measure. (Most of the British North American colonies had two legislative houses. They were governed by what – in appearance at any rate – were real parliaments, small replicas of the Mother of Parliaments in London. The lower house, the Legislative Assembly, was elected on a broad [male] franchise, but the upper house, the Legislative Council, was appointive, and the governor regularly appointed stalwarts of the local oligarchy.) Most romantic reformers argued for elective councils; the strong-minded demanded outright abolition. (Abolition of the upper house is an idea with a long history in this country!)

Some argued for the independent election of the head of the political executive, after the manner of the American president. Many thought the entire Executive Council should be elective. Others argued that the Legislative Assembly should have the power to initiate taxing and spending bills. In short, the rebels wanted more elective offices, and more powers concentrated in the hands of leaders of the assembly. Strong democracy!

But the manifestos and the lists of demands were a kind of façade, a sort of jousting with the liberals on liberal ground. The radicals' true hope was that their threats and proposals would shame or silence the oligarchs and clear away the political, social, and economic factors militating against democracy. Once the old regime had been discredited, a democratic way of life would spontaneously come to light. Many believed that democracy was natural in the New World. The people's collective voice would be heard at last and whatever institutional and constitutional reforms were necessary would follow as a matter of course.

"The people" would speak. "The people" would rise up. The people would say "yea" or "nay." Romantics – some of them at any rate – are not uncomfortable with the idea of consensus. We'll know that we've arrived at democracy when everyone agrees – or everyone except a few recalcitrant political dinosaurs, who can be ignored.

Liberals, in contrast, think of the inhabitants of a political jurisdiction as a diverse lot – an aggregation with different opinions and interests. There's no collective voice. "Grassroots"? asks the liberal. "Collective voice"? Fat chance. Pie in the sky. People speak with one voice only when coerced. What's wanted are political institutions that will express and respect the natural diversity of opinion. We'll know that we've arrived at democracy – if you insist on the word – when freedom of speech, and especially freedom to dissent, is secure.

There is no suggestion that the British North American romantics of the 1830s endorsed a system of party "ins" and "outs." On the contrary, everything points to the idea that Papineau and his supporters expected that once in power they would remain. The "official" and oligarchic parties – by definition not democratic – would be banished forever, and democracy would continue to flow up from the people through the people's party in the Legislative Assembly.

DIVIDED SOULS

Peter J. Smith describes the politics of the Papineau era as an opposition between the party of "virtue" (the party of civic republicanism) and the party of "commerce." In the republican regime, the simple life is the norm; material equality and independent hard work are lauded. Commerce, manufacturing, and the striving for wealth are deplored. Smith is drawing on a model used by historians to depict British and American politics of the eighteenth century. His suggestion that it illuminates vital aspects of the nineteenth century and his use of it to clarify aspects of Canadian history are decidedly novel. His articles, published in the 1980s, received a good deal of well-deserved attention.

There is plenty of evidence in the pamphlet literature of the period to support his contentions and I am in sympathy with the general outlines. Thus, I would argue that what Smith calls the party of "virtue" has its romantic aspects. Of course, the "virtue" that is lauded is not necessarily connected with religious belief. Jean-Jacques Rousseau is the guide, not the Catholic Church. It is a "republican virtue," a secular virtue. The romantics of those days were anti-clerical.

But while I think "virtue" is useful to describe the ideology of the British North American romantics, I reject the idea that the liberals were the party of "commerce" or "wealth." I have already suggested that it's misleading to think of liberalism as an ideology devoted primarily to "who gets what and when." Liberalism usually embraces capitalism but it cannot be seen as the party of a wealthy class. Liberals did not exclude the poor; in the nineteenth century they were at least as active in extending the franchise as romantics. They embraced political equality with fervour. They opposed all suggestion that the wealthy be given special exemptions under law.

In 1829 the American populist Andrew Jackson came to power. In 1832 the Whig government in Britain extended the franchise with the Great Reform Bill. In 1848 the British North American colonies abolished the colonial oligarchies by introducing in the local parliaments the constitutional principle called "responsible government." Responsible government reduced the prerogatives of the colonial governor, requiring him to appoint to his Executive Council only officers who could maintain the confidence of the people's representatives in the Legislative Assembly. But full-blown "power to the people," strong democracy in the romantic definition, did not materialize.

In the end most of the rebels of 1837–38 in British North America accepted responsible government and the new constitutional rules as the better way to protect the rights of the people and the better way to encourage political participation of individuals from all ranks. Louis-Joseph Papineau was one who did. But a few remained recalcitrant; they argued that parliamentary responsible government was just another form of oligarchy, favouring the "few" and demeaning the "many." Democratic hopes had been defeated again. Nothing gold can stay.

The dream of people's democracy did not die altogether,

though for a while it went underground. As I said in Chapter Two the populist parties of western Canada (the Progressives, Social Credit, the CCF) revived the arguments for grassroots direct democracy. Like their predecessors in the mid-nineteenth century, these new democratic parties had the ardour and impatience associated with romanticism but were at the same time determined to find a formula to make democracy "stay." Among the institutions they favoured were the referendum, the initiative, and the recall – familiar still today as features of the Canadian Reform and Alliance parties.

Some aspects of Reform and Alliance indeed echo the old romanticism. They're impatient, and oriented to the future and disenchanted with the past, wary of politics and politicking, and opposed to parliamentary forms of government. But other features of Reform and Alliance are decidedly unromantic. One certainly isn't going to find the Alliance party holding a riot in the streets. They respect property and the economic market's power to generate and distribute wealth. No anti-business sloganeering for them. No trashing of McDonald's and Starbucks!

Nevertheless, like their predecessors in Canadian history, they have the appearance of "divided souls." They distrust institutions but are committed to the search for institutional reform.

THE ANTI-INSTITUTIONAL ROMANTIC

Institutional reform inevitably fails; there is no constitutional formula for democracy. So says the anti-institutional romantic, the romantic whose soul is not divided. Democracy must *always* be more like a rebellion, or revolution – or riot.

The idea is not easy to understand. In discussions with romantics, liberals typically wring their hands and ask, "But just what is it you want? Why can't you be specific? We liberals stand for the rule of law, and representative government, and so on. We're clear about the principles and institutions we believe necessary for good government. But you romantics talk endlessly about democracy without defining it. You don't offer specifics. You're so annoying." (Imagine the Lerner and Loewe lyrics: "Why can't a romantic be more like a liberal? Liberals are so open, so honest, so forthright. Why can't a romantic be more like a liberal?")

Romantics score their points when on the attack. Thus, the romantic will say that an institution like representative government necessarily works to the advantage of men and women who are better educated and wealthier. That's the kind of person who gets elected to a representative assembly. So much for your vaunted liberal rule of law with its supposed principle of equality. With representative government, you liberals have built a bias into the system. You're favouring a particular kind of person. And – no surprise – that kind flourishes under liberal institutions, while others languish. And so it is with all institutions. And all constitutional principles. According to romantics, the confidence in constitutions is liberalism's "dark side."

The romantic believes that institutions, principles, and definitions (insofar as these things are necessary at all) should always be in play, always open to recreation as the people feel the necessity. *That's* democracy. Constitutions especially are suspect. If we romantics laid down a constitution beforehand, we'd be no better than autocrats, no better than you liberals.

5

Are We There Yet? Liberal Arguments

Of course we're there, say the liberals. Parliamentary liberal democracy arrived in England in or about 1688, and in British North America in or about 1848. It's entrenched in the British North America Act of 1867. Canada today is a liberal democracy. (Can our liberal democracy be improved? Probably. I've said that liberals aren't averse to reform. But that's an issue for later chapters.)

What complicates the discussion of "are we there?" is that liberals and romantics invest the word "democracy" with different meanings. Liberals take it for granted that parliamentary government is a form of democracy. Parliamentary government and presidential government are the two forms of liberal democracy. And liberal democracy is "democracy" par excellence. When liberals today speak of "democracy" they are referring to the parliamentary and presidential systems.

Another way to put the issue is to say that liberals don't distinguish between liberalism and liberal democracy. They admit that the parliaments of the early eighteenth century in England had a restricted franchise, and that equality of representation and standards for the distribution of political offices were deficient from our present-day point of view. But they also note that the all-important principles of parliamentary democracy were in place, the representative assembly and systems of responsibility to the House of Commons, the rule of law, and freedom of political speech.

Among political scientists and philosophers today, it's common to make a distinction between liberalism and liberal democracy. The suggestion is that liberalism came first, and liberal democracy followed only later. But the scholars who make this distinction have their own agenda. And it's often a romantic one. Recall the romantic distrust of political institutions, and the romantic propensity to think that society must change before institutions can be reformed. Both notions militate against the idea that liberal democracy took hold as long ago as the eighteenth century.

Romantics don't believe that the parliamentary and presidential systems are *the* two forms of democracy, the only forms. Indeed, they're inclined to think that neither is true democracy. There are other forms of government, other phenomena, more deserving of the term.

In short, liberals and romantics can talk to each other about "democracy" until they're blue in the face without reaching agreement. One can't always tell when or whether they're talking about the same thing.

In the interests of clear thinking and debate (to which liberals are addicted; which they endlessly enjoy, and which they elevate to the high and dignified category of "deliberation" and "the search for truth"), liberals are usually careful to distinguish liberal democracy from what I've been calling romantic democracy or strong democracy.

Romantics, in contrast, let the word "democracy" slip around, partly because they believe definitions and categories are inherently confining (and so "anti-democratic"), but also because they want to inject the good word "democracy" with romantic import. It remains true that when romantics say "democracy" they are not always referring to the presidential and parliamentary systems. That's how the debate went in the twentieth century. We're all familiar with it. How do you like your democracy: "liberal" or "strong"?

In the nineteenth century, essentially the same debate was conducted in a rather different language. No one spoke of "liberal democracy." The term wasn't in the vocabulary. When they wanted to speak of what we now call "liberal democracy," they talked about the English constitution, the British constitution, or the American. Or British traditions and freedoms. British rights. The liberals praised these things, and the romantics – very often – did not.

Nineteenth-century liberals used the term "democracy" to mean mob rule, or a system in which despots professed to speak for the people. On the liberal's lips, "democracy" almost always had this derogatory import. It denoted oppression and tyranny. Nineteenth-century romantics used "democracy" to refer to the grand day when the people would overthrow oppression, the monarchs, aristocrats, and oligarchs went down to defeat, and the people's leaders took office in the people's name.

THE WAY WE WERE

Let's see how that nineteenth-century language plays out in British North American debates.

Insofar as they focused on institutional reform – not always a prime concern for romantics, as I have said, and never the sole concern – liberals and romantics agreed that it was good to encourage political participation. But the romantics (or at least the "divided souls" among them) favoured the introduction of additional elective institutions and offices. To get democracy, go American! We don't have to ask whether they indeed understood the American constitution. They certainly don't appear to have been thinking of a system of "checks and balances" in the style of John Adams or Alexander Hamilton. They sometimes called themselves Jeffersonians, or Jacksonians. But labels like these can be misleading.

The liberals argued for reform of the provincial constitutions to bring them into line with British parliamentary practice. In particular, they wanted the constitutional principle known as "responsible government." To get good government, go British full-strength! As the liberals understood it, this was the issue at the heart of the debates in mid-century British North America. The one side was arguing for more elective institutions and for direct democracy. The other side supported parliamentary responsible government.

It was a fair fight, according to the liberals. And it was a fight the liberals won. By the time of the Confederation debates in the

1860s, everyone or almost everyone had accepted "responsible government."

In the 1830s the romantics leaned heavily on the fact that the government of each colony, that is, the governor and his appointed Executive Council, were nearly impossible to remove from office. Elections came and went but same old gang, the same bunch of oligarchic toadies, would be reappointed to the executive (and to the Legislative Council, the colonial upper house). It didn't matter which party won the majority of seats in the Legislative Assembly, the oligarchy would be back in power. What more proof could you have that the colonial ruling classes and the imperial overlords despised democracy? That's the romantic contention. They were ready with further proof if asked – facts and figures to show that executive councillors (not to mention the legislative councillors, for members of the oligarchy often sat on both councils) were using public funds to enrich themselves and do favours for friends.

But the liberals of the period never questioned these facts and figures. Pierre Bédard, Lord Durham, Joseph Howe, Étienne Parent: these men knew as well as any rebel that the colonies were intolerably oligarchic, and that colonial elites were misusing funds. There was no quarrel on that point. What the liberals argued was that the introduction of responsible government promised the better way of bringing down the oligarchies. The principle of responsible government requires the political executive to answer to the majority of elected representatives in the Legislative Assembly on important legislative measures, especially on all measures involving taxing and the spending of public money. A simple principle? Perhaps. But to hear liberals describe it, it was (and is still today) the sovereign remedy against oligarchy. It expressly forbids uncontested government by a single elite, class, or party.

That's the liberal claim in the nineteenth century. It wasn't necessary to pull some formula for super-democracy out of the future. It wasn't necessary to invent a new constitution or to introduce American-style institutions. British parliamentary practice, responsible government: that's what was wanted. That's also what Durham recommended in his famous Report of 1839. That's what the colonial liberals argued for. It's what was introduced in 1848. And it's what the Dominion of Canada got in 1867.

But why had the British North American colonies been subjected to the wretched rule of the oligarchies in the first place? Why hadn't the full parliamentary system been introduced years before? The answer in a nutshell, as the liberals understood it, was that the colonial executive councils were spending money provided by the British taxpayer. In the first years of the century, the British had reasons to underwrite colonial expenses. There was the matter of defending the colonies against the Americans, for one thing. Defence is always expensive. But the upshot was that the governor could dip into imperial funds to pay his executive councillors. He did not have to submit spending proposals in their entirety to the Legislative Assembly. And that's why the oligarchies remained in power. The people's representatives couldn't vote them out.

Though they tried. Oh, how they tried, and what a marvellous nuisance they made of themselves. There was a shadowy version of responsible government in operation. The governors usually made a show of submitting to the legislative assemblies a budget for monies that had been raised in the province. The assemblies refused salaries whenever they could and some officials went unpaid for months, while assembly members did their best to corner public funds for spending projects of their own devising. It was a glorious, or perhaps inglorious, battle.

According to Durham and the liberals, the great thing was to turn off the imperial money tap or at least reduce it to a drizzle. Each colony should spend on public matters and on government salaries only funds raised in the colony. Thus, all spending, all salaries, would be subject to the assembly vote. The governor would then be required to appoint to the Executive Council men who could maintain the support of that lower-house majority, and all the principal features of the British constitution would fall into place. (Turning off the money tap was the measure Pierre Bédard recommended in 1810 in Lower Canada – the measure that so offended the governor and the local oligarchy in the province that they threw him and some of his colleagues in jail.)

The liberal argument, in brief, was that responsible government would ensure that "the people" at last had an effective voice in public affairs. Government would be conducted always

Are We There Yet? Liberal Arguments   45

with an eye to keeping the support and approval of the people's representatives in the assembly, and, of course, with an eye to the next election. Responsible government was the superior way to include all ranks and all classes in the political process. It was the superior formula for what in the parlance of the next century was called democracy.

I have said that the liberal argument convinced. Individuals who had benefited from the old oligarchic system put away their self-justifying arguments and pronounced themselves converts to "responsible government." (The oligarchs capitulated! How's that for a victory!) The romantics either joined the liberals or sulked in relative obscurity and the romantic argument for elective councils passed into the shadows. The British constitution, rooted in the Revolution of 1688, had triumphed.

But why, you may ask, did the Western parties revive the romantic vision in the twentieth century? The answer is that a new charge was brought against parliamentary liberal democracy. The new complaint was not that the Westminster system did not represent all classes but that it did not represent all regions of the country. And that's a different kettle of fish. Or can of worms.

Let's not open that can at the moment. Let's think rather about what the liberal says to the romantic argument in its full-blown anti-institutional form.

HOW THE LIBERALS RESPOND TO ANTI-INSTITUTIONAL ROMANTICS

Liberals are comfortable when they're quarrelling with romantics who try to make democracy "stay." Defending institutions, fiddling with them, reforming them (in prudent fashion) – it's all grist for the happy liberal. But the romantics who argue that democracy happens, or doesn't, that it wells up like fresh water, that it comes and goes – that contention has the liberals squirming.

The romantic anti-institutional argument says that all permanent political institutions, including the parliamentary system, are suspect because institutions are inherently oppressive. True democracy can't be captured in a constitution or institutional formula. True democracy can never "stay.' It *shouldn't* "stay." Democracy requires a continuing debate about institutions, constitutions, and policy; institutions and principles should always be on the political agenda.

In this argument the liberal feels at a disadvantage. The problems with the romantic formula seem so obvious! How can such a dangerous argument command attention? Surely the romantic is inviting mob rule rather than democracy proper! "Mob rule" means not rule by the masses themselves but rule by strong-willed individuals professing to represent mass demands and on that basis claiming absolute title to govern. Evil Futures threaten.

It's true that the women and men who sit in a representative assembly are likely to be better educated and wealthier than the average citizen, says the liberal. But they are far more likely to act as the servants of the populace than are the self-appointed leaders of mass uprisings and demonstrations. The competition between political parties for seats in the House of Commons and among elites for positions in the government promotes responsiveness. No one governs unchallenged. All must justify their exercise of power by argument, deliberation, and appeal to the sovereign people.

We could choose our parliamentary representatives by lot. Or we could use the sophisticated sampling techniques of the social sciences – the modern improved version of choosing representatives by lot. Sampling techniques would give us a House of Commons that closely mirrored the Canadian population in terms of income, education, ethnic groups, religion, age, and so on. And, in a strict sense, choosing the House of Commons in this fashion would indeed satisfy the liberal principle of equality of each and all under the law. But it's not clear, says the liberal, that such a system would give us representatives more eager to listen to the people and to bring the sentiments of the rank and file into the institutions of government.

Ergo, parliamentary government with its representative and responsible institutions is the superior form of democracy. That's the liberal view.

End of argument? Almost, but not quite. Many who agree that representative and responsible parliamentary institutions are superior nevertheless have their doubts about some features of the parliamentary system in practice, especially (oh dear!) the principle so precious in the eyes of the nineteenth-century champions of liberalism: the principle of "responsible government."

It's said that responsible government today concentrates power unduly in the Prime Minister's Office, the cabinet, and the senior members of the bureaucracy.

As Bill Blaikie, Member of Parliament and long-time advocate of parliamentary reform, says, "The executive is responsible to Parliament. That is the theory of responsible government, and the problem is that it doesn't work that way in practice. The executive directs the legislature rather than being directed by the legislature. There is a sense that the flow of power is going in the wrong direction."

It may be necessary to revisit the quarrel about institutions in British North America. Is it possible we got the democratic formula wrong in 1867?

6

Why Historians Can't Put a Date to Democracy

Canadian historians don't agree on the definition of democracy and don't agree on dates. What's more, they don't address the fact of their disagreement. Democracy – the phenomenon and the issues – are veiled in a cloud of unknowing. From which the conscientious historian averts her eyes.

Historians agree that the constitutional principle known as responsible government arrived in British North America in or about 1848 but only some of them want to think that its introduction entailed democracy. They aren't all of one mind about a date for responsible government in England. They can't say when Britain became a democracy.

In the *Report on the Affairs of British North America*, Lord Durham dates responsible government from 1688: "Since the Revolution of 1688, the stability of the English constitution has been secured by that wise principle of our Government which has vested the direction of the national policy, and the distribution of patronage in the leaders of the Parliamentary majority." But, according to many historians, Durham was wrong. As they tell it, responsible government wasn't established in Britain until, perhaps, 1840. Durham discovered the principle only on his visit to British North America in 1838! The Upper Canadian Robert Baldwin described it to him and he then carried the idea back to Britain. Responsible government was a Canadian invention. (Now that's something to be proud of, eh?)

But wouldn't you think that Lord Durham, famous for describing and recommending responsible government, would know something about its history? He was an experienced parliamentarian. He had been a member of the British House of Commons, and then the House of Lords, and at the time he visited British North America he held a cabinet post in the Whig government. He came from a political family. His father had been a prominent member of Parliament, active in the movement for reform of Parliament in the years before the French Revolution and the Terror. He was well read in the political literature of his day. In other words, he was familiar with parliamentary practice and theory.

Moreover, he was familiar with the romantics of his time. He liked to keep up with groups that described themselves as progressive. He himself had something of a reputation in this area. (He was known as Radical Jack.) Before he left England, he consulted John Arthur Roebuck, Louis-Joseph Papineau's spokesman in the British Parliament, and during his tour of office in the colonies he used Roebuck's arguments to provoke discussion of local grievances. He appointed philosophical radicals (a group of which Roebuck was a charter member) to his research team in 1838, consulted them regularly, and published their findings and some of their opinions in appendixes to the Report. Nevertheless, in the end, despite all his fraternizing with the other side – or because of it, Durham rejected the radical proposal to scrap parliamentary institutions in favour of an up-to-the-minute American-style system. He came down squarely for liberalism and British parliamentary practice. And he argued that British parliamentary practice had its origins in the Revolution of 1688.

The historians' difficulties show in their treatment of Pierre Bédard, thirty years before Durham. Bédard, leader of the majority party in the Legislative Assembly of Lower Canada, described responsible government in the journal *Le Canadien*: "The ministry must necessarily have a majority in the House of Commons. When it loses the influence that has been given to it ... it is relieved." This is how the British constitution has worked for decades, he told his readers, this is how it works in our day, and this is how our colonial constitution should work. (Go directly to jail, M. Bédard. Do not pass go.)

Bédard gets no credit from the historians for describing responsible government. (All the credit goes to the English-speakers, Baldwin and Durham.) He couldn't have been recommending responsible government. It may sound as if he is. (Yes it does!) But no, say the historians, it's too early. Bédard was writing in 1806! Responsible government had not been invented.

So who's right? Bédard (well-read French Canadian notary and parliamentarian)? Durham (famous English parliamentarian and the man on the spot)? Or the twentieth-century scholars? And *why* do the historians have so much trouble accepting the Bédard-Durham version of Canadian history? In *The Transition to Responsible Government*, Phillip Buckner tells the story of the historians' mistake and gives his reasons for concluding that "the essential principle that the ministers of the Crown were responsible to Parliament for the general conduct of the executive was clearly established in the eighteenth century." It would appear that Bédard and Durham were right. But why were the historians wrong (Buckner, for one, excepted)?

DEMOCRACY AND POLITICAL EQUALITY

Part of the answer, I believe, is that the historians don't want to think of England as a democracy from 1688. Thus, those who associate responsible government with liberal democracy are driven to deny that that responsible government came in at the end of the seventeenth century, while those prepared to admit that it arrived at the end of the seventeenth century don't equate it with democracy.

One way or another the historians do some fancy dancing. They sometimes argue that responsible government is a form of liberalism but not liberal *democracy*. Or they admit that it's liberal democracy but suggest that liberal democracy is not, after all, *true* democracy. Consequently, England wasn't democratic in any meaningful sense.

Few Canadian historians reflect on their own assumptions; we have to rely on guesswork. I suggest a principal reason for the historians' difficulty is that they associate democracy with social and material equality and find it hard to detect this kind of equality in eighteenth-century England. And we can surely agree that England in the eighteenth century was a class-dominated society – class-ridden, classist. And so it remained for decades. For centuries, some would argue.

But I believe that, if we fail to see that profound ideas of *politi-*

cal equality were at work in that class-ridden society, if we fail to see that principles of political equality ground the constitution introduced by the Revolution of 1688, we are making a serious mistake. The idea of natural and political equality was out and about and creating trouble in politics long before English society and custom began to exhibit its effects. Indeed, the principle of the "rule of law," which says that no individual, whatever his or her rank (not even kings and queens), can escape the consequences of law or govern outside the law, dates from the Magna Carta of 1215. By the seventeenth century, English politics was alive with arguments for natural equality and speculation about the consequences of this teaching for politics. Thomas Hobbes and John Locke published major books on the subject, books still read and still influential, the ground of our law and politics to this day.

It's politics, not society, that Durham and the colonial liberals are talking about. Durham didn't expect to throw away his title or give away his fortune (though he gave away some of it). At the same time, he did not expect his English constituents to vote him into office because he was Lord High and Mighty. Or even because he was the biggest landlord and employer in the district. He expected to have to convince them by argument. The voters were his equals in this one sense important sense at least, that their political judgments had to be respected. His opinions weren't naturally better or obviously better because he was wealthy and titled.

Durham's idea of an appealing political platform was one that included measures to enhance political equality. In England he campaigned to redraw electoral boundaries to reduce discrepancies in representation; he favoured extension of the franchise and the introduction of the ballot. Moreover, he worked hard to draw into British political life people from the middle and lower classes. In short, he was a typical liberal. The energy he threw into these projects and his openness to novel ideas made some of his contemporaries think of him as a little too romantic. (What's the hurry, Jack?) But a liberal, a liberal democrat, is what he was.

I am arguing that we cannot call "anti-democratic" all societies that lack the degree of social and material equality characteristic of our own time. If we do, we will underestimate the importance of principles of political equality like those that underpinned the

English constitution in previous centuries – and that still support our own. We'll miss the liberalism. And to tell the truth, we won't see the romantic ideology either. We'll miss the liberal-romantic distinction. We'll miss the debate on democracy.

POPULAR SOVEREIGNTY AND EQUALITY IN THE CANADIAN FOUNDING

The historiography of the Confederation period suffers from the same confusions about "democracy" and "equality." It is said, for example, that the Canadian Fathers ignored, or deliberately rejected, the doctrine of popular sovereignty that so clearly underpins the American constitution.

Popular sovereignty powerfully expresses the teaching that all are equal in law. It's like the "rule of law" in this respect. Every individual has the right to life and liberty under law. Every individual is equally entitled to peace, order, and good government. In the formulation familiar from John Locke, popular sovereignty expresses the idea that each and every person subject to a regime must give his or her consent. Every individual must consent.

Of course, in the day-to-day world of politics, as Locke knew – none better – the people's consent is usually expressed by a majority – in extraordinary instances by a referendum majority, in most practical circumstances by the majority or plurality in an election or the majority in the legislature. And there are good reasons why we should be glad that in elections and in parliamentary votes the majority vote determines. Or so the liberal argues. A system of consensus opens the prospect of an oppressive Evil Future, in which minorities are sacrificed on the altar of legitimacy. In liberal democracies, majorities form and reform, as new issues arise, as new party policies and new leaders make their mark. There's no permanent majority, and the hope is always – and it's a hope that is more often realized than not, or so the liberal says – that the transient majorities respect political minorities and political dissent.

At the same time, we should not forget the philosophers' formulation, the idea that *all* must consent. The idea that political majorities should respect minorities itself depends on that underlying, deep-seated idea that each and all consent to be governed.

Why Historians Can't Put a Date to Democracy

Each and all must be respected, and retain their rights and fundamental freedoms, even when they're on the losing side in a vote. The idea of legal equality clings to the doctrine of popular sovereignty. In fact, the two are inseparable. You can't get an order of popular sovereignty without getting the legal equality. That's the liberal argument.

Supposedly, the doctrine of popular sovereignty originated in the seventeenth century and was triumphantly established in the Glorious Revolution of 1688. I've said – or should have – that all modern regimes claim to be grounded in the will of the people. As the American historian Edmund S. Morgan argues, the notion of popular sovereignty can be called an "invention," or a "myth," but it is the invention that has shaped the modern era. It is *our* myth and governs our thinking still today.

Yet Canadian historians and political scientists continue to suggest that the doctrine of popular sovereignty is absent in our history. According to Peter Russell, "at Canada's founding, its people were not sovereign, and there was not even a sense that a constituent sovereign people would have to be invented." Indeed, Russell suggests that, even at the end of the twentieth century, Canadians had only an imperfect understanding. The job was still to be done. The "question of our time" is still this, he argues: "Can Canadians become a sovereign people?"

Talk about Canadian exceptionalism! Canadians very much like to think they're different from the United States, "uniquely" different, perhaps. One sympathizes. This is a dear country. But surely it's going too far to say that our uniqueness consists in the fact that our founders were ignorant of the doctrine of popular consent, a doctrine well-established in John Locke's writings and, according to liberal tradition, perfectly exemplified in the English Revolution of 1688, a doctrine, moreover, that all, liberals and romantics alike, believe present in the American founding. Reading Russell and other political scientists on 1867, one certainly gets the impression that they think the Fathers of the Canadian Confederation were from hicksville.

If there was no understanding of popular sovereignty in the Canadian founding, what follows? Let's take a closer look at those seventeenth-century Enlightenment philosophers. Locke's famous "state-of-nature" teaching depicts savage individuals in early history, free and wild, assembling voluntarily to devise a system of law, a "social contract." As he tells it, each and all agree to give up their natural wildness for the equal constraints of civil society in hope of gaining the security to live out their lives in peace. The story is ludicrous as history, but striking if we take it (as Locke surely intended) as a parable about the equal responsibility of individuals for their lives and welfare, and their equal obligation and equal security under law, in modern liberal regimes.

Romantics have their own version of the original assembly. Rousseau is their teacher, and the whole picture is darker. Rousseau makes the loss of that original wild freedom almost unbearably sad. "All ran to meet their chains," he says in one famous passage. The poor, foolish, wild things, our parents of old, embraced civilization eagerly, thinking to escape the hardships of that early life, thinking that law, or an overlord, offered a remedy. But what followed proved terrible beyond belief. All the wars, the wretched slavery, the concentration camps, and mass slaughters unfold from that original moment of deluded hope. The romantic distrust for government, institutions, and foundations indeed has its beginning in Rousseau.

Nevertheless, Rousseau, as much as Locke, argues that insofar as there is hope for good government, it lies in rigorous insistence on political and legal equality. The chains must weigh on each and all equally. But that such a regime is possible Rousseau believes only from time to time. He's the great teaser. He raises hopes and dashes them, raises them and dashes them. He's a romantic on Mondays, Wednesdays, and Fridays, and an Enlightenment thinker on Tuesdays and Thursdays. The liberal, tutored by Locke, is far more optimistic about possibility of good government and the equality of all under the law.

What we want to remember from the philosophers is that all modern regimes insist on the foundational idea of human equality. And since Locke rather than Rousseau is the philosopher of Canadian Confederation, we should have in mind the liberal teaching especially. Equal citizenship, equal freedom. To say that Canada was not founded on this teaching, or that the Fathers of Confederation only imperfectly recognized it, is to suppose that they approved of inequality, rule by hierarchies, rule by patriarchs and overlords and oligarchs. It suggests they believed there are individuals, and perhaps families, classes, races, tribes, or even political parties, who are naturally – in the very order of creation – entitled to govern other people and to occupy positions of power unchallenged. It suggests that they believed there are natural slaves and natural masters. It suggests, in short, that the Fathers were hostile to ideas of equality that are dear to both romantics (most of them) and liberals.

THE CONFEDERATION DEBATES ON POPULAR SOVEREIGNTY

The contention that the founders ignored popular sovereignty has a certain credibility (not much!) if scholars focus, as they usually do, on the Fathers of Confederation and on the drafting of the British North America Act at the Charlottetown and Quebec conferences of 1864. The document drawn up at Quebec was a no-nonsense affair. Scholars correctly point out that nothing is said directly about popular sovereignty; there's no rhetoric about "we the people." But equally there is nothing in it to admit a teaching about natural hierarchy. The provisions of the Quebec Resolutions and the British North America Act are in every way compatible with natural equality, equal obligation, and equal rights. Indeed, the resolutions and Act *require* equal obligation and equal rights.

The rhetoric about equality, the high philosophical language, surfaces in the legislative debates on Confederation, debates that have been largely ignored in the scholarly literature.

The process of making the Canadian constitution didn't end with the Quebec Conference. The delegates returned from Quebec to put the union proposal to their local legislatures. The rule was simple. The provincial parliaments and assemblies had a veto. No colony could be forced into the union on British say-so or solely at the behest of the colonial elites. There were seven colonies: British Columbia, the Red River settlement (which comes into Confederation as Manitoba in 1870), the United Province of Canada, the three Maritime provinces, and Newfoundland (which votes down Confederation in 1869). After 1867, the colonial legislators were no longer considering the Quebec scheme, of course, but whether to join the Dominion of Canada. Nevertheless, the rule requiring legislative approval held.

In due course, the requisite legislative resolutions were introduced in each colony and lively debates ensued. The Fathers of Confederation, usually sitting on the front benches, had to justify the union deal against considerable opposition. At the Quebec Conference, all had been in favour of union. Disagreements were about ways and means. In the legislative debates a substantial minority was prepared to reject union in any form. Out of that fundamental disagreement comes this question: What process of ratification would make the majority decision legitimate? Thus, the doctrine of popular sovereignty came to the fore.

There were two schools of thought. The one school argued that, if a new nation was in the making, the sovereign people of each colony should vote directly, in a referendum, or in a single-issue election. In Nova Scotia, anti-Confederates opted for popular consultation on the assumption that the sovereign people would reject union. But many Confederates also endorsed the referendum. In the Canadian legislature, where almost everyone was satisfied that the overwhelming majority of people in the province supported Confederation, some members of the legislature nevertheless insisted that direct popular consultation was required to legitimate the deal.

The speakers in this first school have all the best rhetoric. Here is one formulation: "[The] people [is] the only rightful source of all political power." The speaker is James O'Halloran in the Canadian Legislative Assembly in 1865. "When we assume the power to deal with this question [Confederation], to change the whole system of government, to effect a revolution, peaceful though it be, without reference to the will of the people of this country, we arrogate to ourselves a right never conferred upon us, and our act is a usurpation."

In the Nova Scotia House of Assembly (1866), William Lawrence says: the "principle which lies at the foundation of our constitution is that which declares the people to be the source of political power." In the New Brunswick House of Assembly (1866), William Gilbert contends: "[The] only way in which the constitution of a free, intelligent, and independent people can be changed at all is by revolution or the consent of the people."

Gilbert's argument is especially interesting because he links consent of the people with the idea of revolution. In Locke's teaching, popular consent, that is, popular sovereignty, resides always with the people. It legitimates the founding of a regime. It upholds the obligation to obey the law once the regime is founded. But it can be withdrawn, the people can revolt, if the promised security and good government of the social contract is violated "by a long train of abuses." Gilbert is clearly drawing on this Lockean thesis.

But, as I have already argued, they are all Lockeans insofar as they endorse popular sovereignty. The second school of thought is equally in favour of popular consultation, equally sure that the sovereign people must consent to the founding. But it doubts the wisdom of direct consultation in a referendum. The argument is that a referendum yields at best a crude majority. Parliament is the better venue because the parliamentary process is not merely consultative, but deliberative. The formal process of parliamentary debate ensures that all opinion is canvassed and considered. It allows the formation of a well-considered majority.

By a long-standing legal fiction, Parliament is considered to represent everyone inhabiting the country, every last child, woman, and man. Thus, John Mercer Johnson argues in the New Brunswick Assembly in 1866: "The legislature when they meet are the people, and they have ... the power to deal with all questions that may occur during their existence. They are the people for all legislative purposes, and they have the power to change the constitution when they think the country requires it." The rhetoric is a bit flat, but, as we shall see in chapters to come, the underlying argument has considerable force. Parliament supremely has the authority to draw up a new social contract because it is something like the equivalent of that original gathering of wild folk in the state of nature.

So, who's right? The direct-democracy-camp? Or the parliamentarians? There's no need to make up our minds at this point. What's important is that we see popular sovereignty alive, well, and kicking in the Confederation debates. It grounds the idea of equality in our legal system to this day. It grounds our Canadian democracy.

THE RIGHT-CENTRE-LEFT TRAP

Peter Russell suggests that, because the colonists didn't think of themselves as "a people" before they drew up the Quebec

Resolutions and the British North America Act, because the French, the English, and the aboriginals were conscious of themselves primarily as separate groups, or separate "peoples," British North Americans couldn't muster the sense of *collective* sovereignty needed to consent to the new social contract that was Confederation.

But Locke doesn't say that individuals must recognize themselves as "a people" *before* they agree to the social contract (the new constitution). Oh no. Before they agree to the social contract, they're just an aggregation of savage odds and bods. They become "the people" only in and through the act of making the constitution. (Banish thoughts of history from your mind. Banish anthropology. We're talking about Locke's illustrative fairy tale, his "myth," meant to say something about the constitutions of liberal democracies.) The social contract creates "the sovereign people."

Thus, Edmund Morgan argues that the American colonists became "a people" only when the founders agreed to a national legislature, elected by individuals of all the states, making rules for all. At that point, the individuals in the Thirteen Colonies became one (sovereign) people.

Liberal democracy rests on that Lockean idea – "myth" if you want – that the constitution defines the people. Canadians are collectively a sovereign people because we are a national electorate and have a national legislature and other national institutions. Of course, whole groups of us have separate social allegiances and identities. Of course, French and English are always quarrelling. But we maintain those identities and we do that quarrelling as a federation with a national government. We're Canadians, aren't we? Locke would say, "Yes!" He might add, "And long may you enjoy your quarrels."

Let's climb down from the peaks of philosophy. The point is that Russell and other political scientists and historians missed the argument for popular sovereignty in the Canadian founding and missed the arguments for equality and democracy asserted by that doctrine. They were caught by the right-centre-left trap. For whatever reason, they can't help concluding that "democracy" must have a recent date. Democracy, like socialism, happens later in the course of human events – Greek democracy and some other sterling early examples excepted, of course.

Even Phillip Buckner stumbles. He can see that Durham was right to give responsible government an early date. Responsible government dates from 1688 (or sometime not too long after). But Buckner can't accept the idea that responsible government is a form of democracy. No, sir. Parliamentary responsible government may be liberalism of a sort, but it isn't democracy, not *true* democracy. Thus Buckner: "It has long been known that the Fathers of Confederation were not democrats and that they were determined to secure the protection of property and to create barriers against the democratic excesses which, in their minds, had led to the collapse of the American constitution and to the American Civil War."

There is it: the British North America Act is not a prescription for democracy. The BNA Act (now called the Constitution Act, 1867) still regulates our political life in this country. Canadians have made a few amendments to it, and in 1982 created an additional document, the Constitution Act, 1982, which includes the Canadian Charter of Rights and Freedoms. But the Constitution Act, 1867 still describes the form of government that shapes political debate and decision making at the national level. To say the British North Act isn't democratic is to say we aren't a democracy to this day.

7

What Did the Fathers Say?

In defence of historians, it might be argued that it's their job to look at practice rather than principle. They focus on ways in which democratic practice didn't measure up. I suggested above that in Britain especially social customs did not always recognize principles of equality. There were also ways in which political institutions lagged.

Responsible government has two aspects. The first is that the monarch must not meddle in politics. Lord Durham writes: "However partial the Monarch might be to particular ministers or however he might have personally committed himself to their policy, he has invariably been constrained to abandon both as soon as the opinion of the people has been irrevocably pronounced against them through the medium of the House of Commons."

This aspect of responsible government surely dates from 1688 when Parliament ousted James II. But was it always observed? Perhaps not. A strong king or queen could ruffle feathers by threatening to refuse to appoint individuals not approved at court. There was even a little trouble about Durham's appointment to cabinet. In circles close to the court, he was thought of as rather too much of a Frenchie democrat.

The second crucial aspect of responsible government argues that ministries must maintain the support of the majority in the elective house on issues of great important like taxing and spending. Supposedly all members of the elective house are free to deliberate on these issues and thus the cabinet must present reasoned programs and persuasive arguments to the parliamentarians. But in England the use of political patronage for political purposes was far from unknown and members of the commons could be – not to put too fine a point on it – bribed. What happens to the independence of members and to reasoned arguments when great wads of patronage are waved about? Looking at parliamentary *practice* in England in the eighteenth and nineteenth centuries, historians see something less than democracy. And they have an argument. The principle was present; practice hadn't caught up.

There was also the fact that in England the franchise was severely restricted. The Great Reform Bill of 1832 (for which Durham worked so hard) expanded the electorate, but not by much. And there was the problem of the "rotten" boroughs. The situation was somewhat different in British North America. There, the franchise was broad. Voters had to own property, or have an income. But property and wealth were far more equitably distributed in the colonies than in Britain, and almost all adult males could meet the qualifications. (And on occasion, women qualified too! But that's another story.) Was the scramble for patronage less marked in the colonies? Was it less noticeable after the introduction of responsible government?

The point is that, when we look at practice alone, the nineteenth-century parliamentary system was deficient in the democracy department. Yet, at the same time, there were always those principles, those strong arguments for equality under the law and for the necessity of securing popular consent, tugging at the conscience of legislators, political observers, and the public. Practice is always imperfect. All human institutions are flawed. What we really want to know is whether the *principles* of parliamentary government deserve the accolade "democracy."

Consider again Phillip Buckner's contention: "It has long been known that the Fathers of Confederation were not democrats and that they were determined to secure the protection of property and to create barriers against the democratic excesses which, in their minds, had led to the collapse of the American constitution and to the American Civil War." The Fathers were "determined to secure the protection of property." Whose property? Their own? Undoubtedly. But only their own? Buckner associates property rights with an anti-democratic bias. He supposes that the Fathers meant to secure the wealth of the "haves," the class of people like themselves, from the depredations of "have-nots." But, if I'm right in saying that the underlying principles of the British constitution support equality, what's sauce for the goose is sauce for the gander. Under the rule of law and the principles of natural equality, laws that protect the grand estates of the rich will also protect the little bits of land and the small savings of the poor. It's far from clear that security for property rights is *ipso facto* anti-democratic.

We know from Hernando de Soto that states in which the poor have no secure title to their property experience grinding poverty generation after generation. Without titles and records, individuals and families can do little to protect themselves against thieves and bullies. They can't invoke the protection of the police or assert their claims in court. They can't protect themselves against the rich! Just as important in de Soto's view is that they can't sell "their" land and or raise mortgages. Thus, there's no way to assemble capital for small businesses or for education, no way of lifting their children out of despair (short of theft, joining the bullies, raiding neighbours).

Security for property rights was a concern in many British North American colonies. Prince Edward Island struggled with its absentee landlords. Lower Canada embarked on reform of the seigneurial tenure. In his 1839 Report, Durham argues at length that the inadequate systems of land tenure and registration in the Canadas, and the arbitrary distribution of land grants, had had adverse consequences for immigrants, for small landholders, and for the prosperity of the society as a whole. Like so many in his time (and like de Soto today), Durham was convinced that good laws and good institutions promote prosperity. And by "good" laws he meant laws that protect each and all equally. He was struck by the relative prosperity of the United States. In his opinion, the economic stagnation of the Canadas was proof of poor laws and poor administration.

During the twentieth century it was often argued that the economy drives legislative reforms, institutional reform – and revolution. Wall Street rules. Bay Street rules. Today, this notion lingers. But Durham was not acquainted with Marx. He believed that the politicians were in the driver's seat. If a population was poor, politicians and the political institutions should be held accountable. Turn out the offending party! Repeal or reform the laws!

Property rights don't eradicate differences between rich and poor. But they do open opportunities for the accumulation of property by persons in every class – "the country man at plough" as much as "the favourite at court." And if Durham and de Soto are right, they raise the standard of living across the board. Property rights benefit the poor. And so the protection of property in law and in the constitution can be considered anti-democratic only if democracy is defined as a system of material equality.

Buckner has other arguments. He says, for example, that the Fathers erected "barriers" against democracy. What barriers? They "limited the size of the House of Commons so that it would remain manageable," he contends. They "chose to have an appointed rather than an elected second chamber, and sought to ensure that both houses of the proposed federal legislature were composed of men who possess a substantial stake in society."

What is being suggested here is that the Fathers intended to run Parliament and to manage the nation's business to suit themselves as class: they intended to protect their "stake in society" at the expense of the *demos*. The argument, in brief, is that the Constitution Act, 1867 entrenches oligarchy. The ruling cliques, the Family Compact, the "official" parties were not banished with the introduction of responsible government in 1848. They flourished after 1867 under other names. They may be flourishing still today, because of the Fathers of Confederation.

WHAT THE FATHERS SAID

The preamble of the British North America Act states that the new general legislature of the union is to have a form of government "similar in principle to that of the United Kingdom." Textbooks usually suggest that this phrase, "similar in principle," indicates that the parliamentary form of government, including the principle we know as responsible government, was to be adopted by the Dominion of Canada as a constitutional convention. (Constitutional conventions look like constitutional law and feel like constitutional law but are not spelled out in a constitutional document; the courts cannot enforce them.) Responsible government is sometimes said to be *the* prime example of a constitutional convention. It's the definitive principle of parliamentary democracy but in our founding document gets only a wave of the hand: "similar in principle." How extraordinary that such an important feature of the constitution has this airy-fairy foundation! How extraordinary that even "written" constitutions in the British tradition rely so much on "unwritten" foundations! So the texts often read. But let's see.

Section 17 of the BNA Act states that the Parliament of Canada consists of the queen, the Senate, and the House of Commons. It's quite usual to take the term "Parliament" as the equivalent of "House of Commons," but the constitution says otherwise. Parliament consists of *three* elements – or branches, as they're sometimes called – the queen and the two legislative houses. Policy does not become law without the approval of all three.

Earlier sections in the BNA Act define the role of the queen. Section 12 says that the governor general of Canada acts for the queen, and section 13 says that the governor general acts by and with the advice of the queen's Privy Council for Canada. In other words these two sections, especially 13, enshrine that crucial first aspect of responsible government I referred to above: The Monarch Shall Not Meddle Directly in Politics.

The monarch (or his/her representative) *has* the power but does not *wield* it, except on advice. What's the point of this convoluted piece of constitutional mumbo-jumbo? Is it just a leftover from the past? I would argue that it's much more important than that! And if we ever lose it we'll be very sorry. But let's skip the full account of the monarch's role for the time being.

Who is the Privy Council, the all-important giver of advice without whom the monarch does not act (or perhaps acts only in exceptional instances)? The council is a sort of honorary who's-been-who of Canadian politics. Appointments to the council are for life but its effective part is one committee – the group of men and women who comprise what's commonly known as the cabinet, or the government of the day. Now recall the second crucial aspect of responsible government. As we defined it above, with a little help from Pierre Bédard and Lord Durham, the cabinet is appointed by the monarch (on advice), always on the understanding that it will be able to command the support of the majority of the members in the House of Commons on measures of signal importance. Where's that written?

Here we have to think about what entitles governments to take and spend Canadians' money. When your neighbour reaches into your pocket or bank account for funds to spend on projects of his own devising, we call it theft. He can go to jail. When governments do it we say that it is constitutionally justified. We may think the tax rate too high. And we're free to complain about that. We may object to the government's spending priorities. We can complain again. But if we attempt to withhold the money, *we* end up in jail. The argument is that we, through our representatives in Parliament, agreed to the levy.

The crucial sections of the 1867 constitution are 53 and 54. Section 53 says that money bills – that is, bills for appropriating "any part of the public revenue," or for imposing "any tax or impost" – must "originate" in the House of Commons. The section is sometimes interpreted to mean that money bills must not be given first reading in the Senate; they must be debated first in the popular house. This interpretation is good, but it does not go far enough. The all-important consequence of section 53 is quite simply that money bills must be debated by the House of Commons. The Commons cannot be ignored. The government can't raise (or spend) money without the approval of the people's elected representatives. In short, section 53 entrenches the principle, familiar from British history and American rhetoric, of: "no taxation without representation"! Wars have been fought in defence of it.

Section 54 supplies the limitation on the "no taxation" principle that distinguishes parliamentary systems from presidential ones. The House of Commons may consider only those money bills recommended to them by "message of the Governor General" (a.k.a. cabinet). Backbenchers in the Commons, and Senators, cannot draw up and present to Parliament legislative proposals for taxing and spending. That's the job of the Privy Councillors we call the cabinet. It's because of section 54 that the Commons is presented with a coherent program of spending and taxing legislation rather than a shopping list of competing demands from individual representatives.

Before 1848, the British North American colonies were without the principle, or practice, that's today enshrined in section 54. Lord Durham was shocked by the "scramble for local appropriations" that resulted from its absence. In what I've said so far about the Durham Report, I've stressed Durham's disapproval of the oligarchies – the parties ensconced in the colonial executive and legislative councils. The oligarchies were spending money without the approval of the people's elected representatives in the legislative assemblies. A very grievous fault! (Now, of course, it is outlawed, by section 53.)

But Durham had some harsh words for the members of the legislative assemblies too. He was harshest about their attempts to wrest from the Executive Council responsibility for drafting spending bills and introducing them in the legislature. The people's parties in the local assemblies had managed to corner at least some sources of revenue and individual members appeared before the assembly with lists in hand. In effect, such matters as famine relief, roads, and schools became political loot, up for grabs. The Durham Report's appendix on education, for example, notes though there was a general desire for a publicly funded school system in Lower Canada, the province had great difficulty establishing one – owing to the lack of the crown prerogative. Schools opened and closed, and were provided or not provided with books, according to the fortunes of political parties in area, the party affiliation of the teacher, and energies of the local member of the Legislative Assembly.

Wresting spending from the oligarchic parties and locating responsibility for drafting budgets squarely in the popular house was a large part of the radical program of the 1830s. They had no doubt it was more democratic. After all, who was closest to the people? Who knew their needs better? Not the toadies and stuffed shirts in the Legislative and Executive Councils, the men who put themselves forward for promotion by the crown! But Durham did *not* think that control of spending by the Legislative Assembly was democratic. That the provinces adopt the essential crown prerogative was one of his major recommendations and he describes it as a principle constantly exercised in Great Britain for "the real protection of the people." Canadians today are protected by section 54.

The effect of sections 53 and 54 is that neither the cabinet nor the House of Commons can tax or spend independently. The Commons, relying on 53, scrutinizes bills and indeed has every incentive to scrutinize; it may reject cabinet's proposals, but it cannot take the initiative. The Commons does not govern. It's the cabinet that takes the initiative, because of section 54. The cabinet governs, but it cannot act without the people's approval through their elected representatives. Voilà! Responsible government.

Despite what textbooks say, responsible government and thus parliamentary democracy is entrenched in central clauses of the Constitution Act, 1867. Why should we be surprised? The Fathers were familiar with responsible government in their parliamentary legislatures. They knew the colonial history. If they forgot it, they refreshed their memories by reading the Durham Report. Clearly, the two money-bill sections of the 1867 act reflect their understanding of the unsatisfactory operation of the provincial parliaments before responsible government. They inserted section 53 to prevent the rise of Family Compacts in new form. They inserted section 54 to restore authority to the colonial executive, to prevent the "unseemly scramble for local appropriations" among assembly members, and to curb the excesses of strong "democracy."

WHAT MACDONALD SAID

We've seen that cabinet and Commons each have constitutionally prescribed powers. In the nineteenth century it was usual to speak of the "independence" of Parliament's three branches, the cabinet and the two legislative houses, or even of a "separation of powers." This usage continued after the introduction of responsible government. It was not uncommon even in the first decades of the twentieth century.

Later in the twentieth century, political scientists began to speak of a "fusion" of executive and legislative powers in the parliamentary system and this is now standard usage. It's said that the American constitution is characterized by the separation of powers and that Britain and Canada have "fused" powers. So goes the argument in the textbooks.

It is easy to see how this usage came about. In the United States members of the cabinet may not have seats in the legislature. In Canada they must have seats in the legislature. But though in parliamentary systems cabinet and the legislature are inseparable, they are distinguishable in constitutional law, and a good deal hangs on this fact.

The notion of "fusion" completely obscures the cabinet-Commons distinction we have found in the 1867 act. And on that distinction, liberals like Macdonald argue, depend the political freedoms of parliamentary democracy. Parliament is not monolithic. Because it is required by the principle of responsible government to maintain the support of the majority in the Commons, the cabinet represents only one political party or a coalition of parties. It can never claim to represent all shades of political opinion in the country. It can never claim to represent the nation *in toto*. The House of Commons is the branch of parliament with the best claim to represent the country. But, as we have seen, the Commons does not govern.

Though the majority in the Commons usually supports the government, there is always a recalcitrant minority in the house dissatisfied with cabinet's program, and the fact of that recalcitrant minority is a vivid, effective witness – an entrenched witness – to freedom of political speech and the people's right to dissent, to oppose their rulers, and to organize with a hope of ousting them. Citizens must obey laws passed by the majority of the day, but there is no requirement that they approve of those laws. Quite the contrary. And, owing to the marvellous mechanism of sections 53 and 54 in the Constitution Act, their right to be dissatisfied is secure and honoured as the expression of a loyal opposition.

Here's John A. Macdonald on the parliamentary system. He is speaking in the Legislative Assembly of the Province of Canada in the Confederation debates of 1865, describing the form of government that will obtain at the national level in the new federation: "We will enjoy here that which is the great test of constitutional freedom – we will have the rights of the minority respected. In all countries the rights of the majority take care of themselves, but it is only in countries like England enjoying constitutional liberty, and safe from the tyranny of a single despot or of an unbridled democracy, that the rights of minorities are regarded." By the "minority," and "the minorities," Macdonald does not mean ethnic or religious minorities, as some commentators have supposed. He means political minorities, the political opposition in the legislature and in the electorate and public at large. The singular advantage of parliamentary government is that the majority cannot claim to *be* the nation. It is compelled to refrain from riding roughshod over the minority, that is, over dissenting political opinion.

The separation of powers inherent in the principle of responsible government divides political elites. It prevents them from cosying up in a governing oligarchy. It pits them against each other, forcing them – as they hope to satisfy their ambition for office – to compete for popular support.

YES, YES, BUT IS IT DEMOCRACY?

Parliamentary responsible government recognizes popular sovereignty. It protects political minorities. It guarantees freedom of political speech. When coupled with almost any system of free elections – even a system with a restricted franchise – it enables recourse against unpopular rulers. Do we now have a sufficient definition of democracy?

It may be that Buckner's charge still has some force. Parliamentary responsible government is anti-oligarchic to a degree that he does not recognize. But is it democratic? Two lines of argument suggest themselves. It can be said first that, though parliamentary government is a form of democracy, it's not strong democracy. It's not the true, romantic *thing in itself*. Let's put aside this issue for the time being.

The second line of argument is one even liberals might acknowledge. And it's one I've raised before. Responsible government may be less successful in preventing oligarchy than I have made out. It has the *appearance* of a system opposed to oligarchy. It is designed to oppose oligarchy. But in practice matters sometimes work out differently. The concentration of political initiative in the hands of cabinet sometimes, perhaps often, tends to perpetuate unduly the authority of the party in office.

We're at the heart of the debate between liberals and romantics in nineteenth-century British North America. We must take another look at John A. Macdonald's rhetoric. What exactly does he mean by "unbridled democracy"?

8

The Monarchical Element

Listen again to John A. Macdonald in the 1865 Confederation debates: "In all countries the rights of the majority take care of themselves, but it is only in countries like England, enjoying constitutional liberty, and safe from the tyranny of a single despot or of an unbridled democracy, that the rights of minorities are regarded."

Few of Canada's founders praise "democracy," and some have very harsh things to say about it. Macdonald says "unbridled democracy" leads to a despotism. In the same debate, George-Étienne Cartier contends that "democracy" imperils civil peace:

We found ourselves at the present day discussing the question of the federation of the British North American provinces, while the great federation of the United States was broken up and divided against itself. There was, however, this important difference to be observed in considering the action of the two peoples. They [the Americans] had founded a federation for the purpose of carrying out and perpetuating democracy on this continent; but we, who had the benefit of being able to contemplate republicanism in action during a period of eighty years, saw its defects, and felt convinced that purely democratic institutions would not be conducive to the peace and prosperity of nations.

"Purely democratic institutions [are] not conducive to the peace of nations." Undoubtedly this kind of language has made it easier for historians to conclude, as Philip Buckner does, that the Fathers "were not democrats." Cartier continues: "We were not now discussing the great problem presented to our consideration in order to propagate democratic principles. Our attempt was for the purpose of forming a federation with a view of perpetuating the monarchical element. The distinction therefore between ourselves and our neighbours was just this: in our federation the monarchical principle would form the leading feature, while on the other side of the lines, judging by the past history and present condition of the country, the ruling power was the will of the mob, the rule of the populace." At the time, the American Civil War was still in progress. Cartier clearly believed the American federation was in jeopardy. And he was not alone. Historians often point out – correctly – that some Fathers, Macdonald especially, argued for allocating strong powers to the federal level of government in order to prevent the kind of secessionist tendencies that were evident south of the border. But note that in the passages just cited, Cartier is not discussing the division of legislative powers in the British North American federation. He is not suggesting that a weak general government will invite secessionist wars. He is saying that *democracy* invites war.

There's no need to make a mystery of such statements. Macdonald and Cartier are inveighing against the form of democracy we have been calling strong or romantic. Both staunchly defend parliamentary responsible government. If we believe parliamentary government is liberal democracy, then we must conclude that the Fathers *are* democrats – democrats as we use the word in our own day.

The argument is that the new general government of the colonial union will not be, and should not be, "purely" democratic. It should not be an "unbridled democracy." When they raise the spectre of tyranny, when they deplore mob rule, Macdonald and Cartier are remembering the democratic excesses that led to the despotisms of Cromwell and Robespierre, and the threat posed by Papineau's defence of a perpetually governing people's party. They remember evil pasts and they call up the prospect of Evil Futures.

It has been easier for commentators to ignore the substance of Macdonald and Cartier's thought because they were Conservatives. In the right-centre-left scheme, conservatism is always on the point of becoming irrelevant. Macdonald and Cartier were not advanced thinkers even in their day. So argues right-centre-left. And at Confederation their day was more or less over. Their arguments would soon be of antiquarian interest only. "The Moving Finger writes; and having writ,/ Moves on." The future; we must always look to the future! That's the message of right-centre-left. Supposedly even the capital-l Liberals were nearing their best-before date.

Nevertheless it is important to note that in the drafting of the Confederation deal, Liberals were as influential as Conservatives. Confederation wasn't the product of the Conservatives alone. Far from it. Liberals of great ability, like George Brown and Oliver Mowat, were always at Macdonald's elbow, ever on guard to see that Liberals in all the colonies would be able to live with the new regime, reminding him of what he surely knew, that a liberal political constitution must not favour one political party or ideology.

It is true that the Conservatives more often use language that to our ears has an archaic quality. When Macdonald summons a picture of "the single despot," when Cartier praises "the monarchical element," they are employing the language of "mixed government." The terms are as old as the seventeenth century, or older. The Liberals sound more up to date. We won't find Brown raising the spectre of "the single despot." He doesn't use phrases like "unbridled" democracy. But, as I shall argue, the Liberals as much as the Conservatives regard parliamentary government as a "mixed" form of rule. Brown is wary of advocating measures that would detract from the powers of the House of Commons. But he is no friend of strong democracy. He, too, wants to see democracy bridled, in order to protect political minorities.

It's time to explore this seemingly antique notion of the mixed regime.

MIXED GOVERNMENT

The categories are three: monarchy, aristocracy, and democracy. The rule of the "one," the "few," and the "many." It is a scheme or model as old as Aristotle. Everyone who takes an introductory political science course makes its acquaintance, if only briefly, usually in the chapter on Greece. Aristotle believed that the three forms in their "pure" state were easily corrupted. Monarchy declines to tyranny. Aristocracy becomes self-serving oligarchy.

The Monarchical Element

And democracy opens the door to licence, self-indulgence, and anarchy. His remedy? A constitution that combined the three regimes: mixed government.

How are we to think of this threefold scheme in relation to our liberal-romantic dichotomy? Let me suggest that in general liberals support mixed government. Romantics do not. Romantics hanker for the pure forms.

If there were still pure monarchies today, romantics, or some of them, would be monarchists. If there were real aristocracies, they'd embrace glamorous ideas of hierarchy and deference, honours, battle, and glory. In their dreams perhaps, and in their choice of reading materials some are still monarchists, still loyal followers of dukes, princes, clan chiefs, and brave warlords. Think of the success of the field of fiction called "sword and sorcery"! In some distant galaxy the House of Atriedes still rules, in Middle Earth Aragorn rules, and each commands the hearts of millions, romantics all, at least while the story is fresh in the mind.

But in the gritty world today, all political regimes acknowledge popular sovereignty. The choice today is between pure democracy (strong democracy) and mixed government, that is, liberal democracy. Thus, romantic enthusiasm gravitates to pure democracy while liberal prudence suggests the mixed form, the bridled form, democracy constrained by institutional guarantees, checks and balances, and the rule of law.

Aristotle's philosophy of mixed government dominated political science until well into our own period. The history is too long to recount in detail here. In the ancient world, Polybius gives an influential account. In the early modern period, Machiavelli describes Roman history in terms of the Aristotelian model (with a Machiavellian spin). And so it passes into seventeenth- and eighteenth-century French and English political philosophy. Montesquieu offers two versions. The first describes the three functions of government: executive, legislative, and judicial. This model is still invoked on occasion when an author wants to remind us of the importance of "judicial independence" (the principle that calls on politicians and parties to refrain from attempting to influence judges, and that calls on judges to stay out of politics).

The second version, also found in Montesquieu, describes the legislative function as a mixed form. Thus it's said that the English Parliament, the legislative power in the English constitution, is itself an example of mixed government. This is the argument that regards the English Parliament as a combination of the monarchic element (the crown, and the ministers of the crown, that is, the cabinet), the aristocratic element (the upper legislative chamber, in England, the House of Lords), and the democratic element, the House of Commons.

French-speakers in British North America, like Pierre Bédard and Etienne Parent, were familiar with Montesquieu on England. They also read Blackstone, Edmund Burke, and other British constitutional lawyers. The English speakers in the colonies were less likely to know Montesquieu but were well versed in the British tradition. Both French and English read Jean-Louis de Lolme's *The Constitution of England*, first published in London in 1776 and still being reprinted in the 1850s. De Lolme is an ardent supporter of the mixed regime and a lively writer. (But who reads him today? There are a few copies of *The Constitution of England* in old archives. There are no readers. De Lolme is one of Canada's forgotten mentors.)

One point must be made. Ancient mixed government (as Aristotle and Polybius describe it) presupposes principles of inequality. The argument is that the mixed regime will accommodate, and take advantage of, the natural superiority of the one and the few – the natural strength of the kingly, the natural virtue of aristocrats. It was said to be one purpose of good political institutions to enable the better sorts of men to flourish, according to their type. The democratic element, the people, the "many," should be accorded a place in the scheme, but perhaps only for prudential reasons; their exclusion would rankle and might lead to disobedience or revolution. Thus, ancient mixed government had a democratic "element" but was not itself a form of democracy.

Mixed government in modern dress (from the seventeenth century) jettisons all notion of natural superiority as a requirement for citizenship or the right to govern. It fully incorporates the modern philosophy of natural human equality. I am not saying that modern mixed government fails to notice that some persons are naturally stronger, more able, intelligent, ambitious, dastardly, or cruel. The contention is that, in the strict terms of law and citizenship, these qualities should not matter. The law does not "see" your natural endowment, birth, wealth, religion, or tribe. Or it should not. If the penalty for the crime is imprisonment, the strong man pays and the weak one is not excused. The law respects the poor man's property just as it respects the rich man's. Or it should. That's the principle. It is flouted in practice all too often no doubt, but, all the same, it is always lurking, always compelling attention. Law restrains even the monarch.

What is retained from the ancient formula is the idea that there are three forms of government, that each is open to corruption, and that a combination of the three is best. In one of his first speeches in the Canadian Assembly on Confederation, John A. Macdonald assured the house that the general government of the new federation would replicate the British system of "King, Lords, and Commons." In 1869 Newfoundland's F.B.T. Carter argued that the government of the new Dominion was composed of "those three estates to which [Newfoundlanders] were already so well accustomed – the monarch, the Senate, and the House of Commons, elected by the people." When Carter made this speech, Newfoundland had still not made its final decision on Confederation; he was attempting to appease the anti-Confederates.

Each branch is prone to corruption; each dreams of aggrandizement and power. But because they form part of a single system, each branch must watch the others, checking imprudence and haste and reigning in the ambitions of political elites. The importance of the Senate now comes to light. It has the task of delaying or obstructing legislation when it appears that cabinet is attempting to use its majority in the Commons to silence dissent and suppress minorities. The two legislative houses together prevent the cabinet from highhandedness, while cabinet and Senate discourage leaders in the Commons from demagogic posturing.

Evil pasts! Evil Futures! If the monarchic branch dominates unchecked, we'll suffer ills like those that characterized the age of absolutism in the seventeenth century; we'll once again be subject to the bullying and overweening arrogance of "kingly" despots who pretend to have God in their pockets, Stuarts and Bourbons in modern suits and tie. If the "aristocratic" branch dominates, we'll see a return to offensive oligarchies like those that ruled in British North America in the 1830s. Or so goes the theory. If the democratic branch gains the upper hand (unlikely in present-day Canada, but twentieth-century history shows how often it has happened in modern nations, alas), we'll be the playthings of demagogues and populist despots who claim absolute authority to speak for the nation, for the people, for History, for the Future.

To do the work of checking, each branch or element must have a degree of constitutional independence. I've already argued that the "monarchic" and the "democratic" branches of government are supported by different sections of the Constitution Act, 1867. Indeed, these branches are surprisingly "independent." Pierre Elliott Trudeau was notorious for saying that, a few yards from the House of Commons, members were "nobodies." He meant the remark to demean MPs. But in strict terms of law, he was right. When Parliament rises, the members of the Commons retain no powers of government to distinguish them from ordinary citizens. If ordinary citizens are nobodies (not!), then members of the Commons when Parliament's out are nobodies. Senators are also nobodies, in this sense, when Parliament's out. Cabinet members, in contrast, retain the powers that go with the prerogatives of the crown (though not the legislative powers they enjoy as members of the Commons or Senate). The executive government does not come to a halt when Parliament rises.

John Locke thought the fact that members of the legislative houses were "nobodies" when Parliament was not sitting was one of the great guarantees of political freedom and good government in the English system. The members had to go home periodically, to live under the laws they themselves had promulgated. The point is worth thinking about. We'd be in a pickle if we had a permanently sitting body of legislators. So Locke argues, at any rate. (Remember John Mercer Johnson's statement that the "legislature when they meet are the people." Johnson had it right. They're the people "when they meet." And only when they meet.)

That the American presidential system is also a mixed regime I hardly need to say. Scholars feel more comfortable using the language of mixed government of the U.S. system for reasons I have given. Certainly political scientists use "separation of powers" to describe the presidential form of government, because the American president and his cabinet do not have seats in the legislature. But it is correct to use the term "separation of powers" in reference to the British system, too, as I argued in the last chapter. The three branches in the Canadian system may not be *as* "separate" as the branches in the u.s. system. But they have an important degree of independence from each other. The cabinet does not speak for the whole of the House of Commons. The House of Commons may not usurp cabinet prerogatives. The Senate is "independent" again. It cannot be ignored, and is another check in the delicate parliamentary system of "checks and balances."

DREAMS OF THE RED CHAMBER

It may surprise readers that, in the debates on Confederation, Liberal members were more inclined than Conservatives to support an appointive Senate. You'll remember that Phillip Buckner believes the choice of an appointive Senate was a sign of the founders' anti-democratic bias. But it's George Brown the Liberal, not John A. Macdonald the Conservative, who argues at length for appointment. Macdonald defers to Brown on the issue of Senate appointment but makes it clear that he would have been just as happy with a system of election.

Brown's position is this: an elective upper chamber would have more legitimacy with the people than an appointive one and might thus be in a position to compete with the House of Commons for the right to veto money bills. Brown is jealous of the powers of the Commons – the democratic house – and proud of the achievement of responsible government. He argues for retaining a second legislative house; he is not in favour of abolition. He believes that the new Senate will supply a necessary check on the ambitions of cabinet and Commons and will help to reign in autocratic first ministers. But it must not be so strong that the electoral house – the Commons – is cowed.

The whole marvellous structure of parliamentary mixed government, the executive branch and the two legislative houses, is meant to prevent any one individual, faction, clique, or party from monopolizing power. Does it always work? There have been long periods in Canadian history when it appeared to work only imperfectly. But if we consider the liberal democracies of all kinds, parliamentary and presidential – all of them deriving from the old philosophy of mixed government – it surely has to be said that no other system protects so well against the single tyrant, the stubborn oligarchy, and leaders who use populist credentials to claim uncontested right to rule in perpetuity.

POLITICAL DELIBERATION AND POPULAR SOVEREIGNTY

What I have said so far could be taken to mean that parliamentary liberal government – as a system of "checks" – is primarily a means to stop governments from taking actions that intrude in the private sphere of freedom. It is a good system for a minimal state, perhaps, the so-called "night watchman state" in which the government of the day is expected to do little more than maintain civil peace, enforce contracts, and protect citizens from terror and external invasion, though it may not be as good for a welfare state.

But advocates of the parliamentary system make a bolder claim. They argue that a system that protects the political minority, that honours free political speech, will give rise to the kind of deliberation that enables the development of projects of law and policy in the national interest. It is not necessary to suppose that the mixed regime works best only in the minimal state. It will enable governments to embark on programs to redistribute wealth among regions and among citizens and other projects of the political imagination. Of course by the same argument, Parliament is also a good arena for contesting such programs.

The important point is that, after the introduction of responsible government, Parliament became an effective arena of deliberation on projects for the common good. Indeed, the nineteenth century as a whole might be called the Great Age of Political Deliberation. The political actors and the public had a confidence in the power of words unmatched in our own time.

JUSTICE DUFF'S FANCY FLIGHT OF LOGIC

The importance of parliamentary deliberation is described by Chief Justice Lyman Poore Duff in the Alberta press case of 1938, in which the Supreme Court of Canada struck down a provincial statute restricting freedom of the press. Duff maintained that, in restricting freedom of speech, the Alberta legislature had contravened the provisions of the British North America Act. The careful reader will wonder where in the BNA Act freedom of speech is guaranteed. Indeed, there is no such provision in plain language. There is, however, that clause in the preamble to say that the constitution of the Dominion of Canada is to be similar in principle to that of the United Kingdom. From this point Duff's logic takes off. The constitution of the United Kingdom was a parliamentary democracy. Thus, we may say that the 1867 Act established a parliamentary democracy in this country. Moreover, Duff goes on – add a bit of blue sky here – parliamentary democracies require freedom of speech. Ergo: the British North America Act requires freedom of speech:

The [BNA Act] contemplates a parliament working under the influence of public opinion and public discussion. There can be no controversy that such institutions derive their efficacy from the free public discussion of affairs, from criticism, from attack upon policy and administration and defence and counterattack; from the freest and fullest analysis and examination from every point of view of political proposals. This is signally true in respect of the discharge by Ministers of the Crown of their responsibility to Parliament, by members of Parliament of their duty to the electors, and by the electors themselves of their responsibilities in the election of their representatives.

Parliaments depend on free speech; it's the breath of life to them. In effect, a legislature that attempts to restrict free speech is acting in un-parliamentary fashion. We might even say that, insofar as the Alberta legislature retained its parliamentary character, it hadn't passed the offensive law – not really. We can treat the "law" as if it never existed. It's null and void. What a piece of legal foo-fah-rah, eh?

The other judges in the case found a straightforward way to get rid of the law. They said that it fell within the criminal law power of the federal level of government. Only the federal level could pass a law with the criminal sanctions described in the Alberta Press Bill. There. Job done. Offensive law scotched. No need to fool around with complicated philosophical questions and fancy logic.

I feel some sympathy for both sides. In general, it's probably better for courts to rely on well-known precedents and to follow familiar lines of argument. Excursions into the wilds of philosophy – especially philosophy about the nature of legislatures – invite trouble. They lead to questions about the wisdom of our political system. And questions about the wisdom of our system invite principled disobedience. They have a place in the classroom. But perhaps not in the courts. Nevertheless, Duff's argument shows a sterling understanding of parliamentary liberal democracy. We learn from Duff that, without free speech, there is no parliament. A governing council where freedom of speech doesn't operate isn't a parliament. It's – what? The tyrant's support group? The tyrant's bunch of toadies? And by the same logic, where there are parliaments, there's a – sort of – guarantee of free speech, one that's probably as good as anything one will find in a formal bill of rights. I like this argument and I think it's true. We can give it a simpler formulation: rights flourish in liberal democracies (and wither in autocracies).

The Alberta press case is interesting for another reason. Notice that the majority finds itself saying that the offensive law would be constitutional if passed by the federal level under the criminal law power. Of course, the suggestion is – ha! ha! – that the federal parliament would never do such an unfortunate thing. (Why not? The judges don't say.)

The tidy minds in Canadian law were unhappy with the use of the sections of the constitution describing the division of legislative powers to determine rights cases. They liked Duff's dodge even less. And so the idea took hold that Canadians should have a properly entrenched bill of rights, adjudicated by the courts. Unfortunately, in the excitement of adopting a Charter of Rights and Freedoms, Canadians forgot Duff's teaching entirely. We forgot that parliaments have an interest in securing rights. We began to think of parliaments as tyrants, ever ready to trespass on the citizen's liberties, to invade the sphere of private rights. And we began to think of the courts and the courts alone as guardians of our precious rights and liberties.

9

Parliament: The Talking Shop

Canadian scholars only sometimes admit that Locke influenced the Canadian founding. When they do admit it they usually suggest that we didn't get him full-strength. Especially, it's said, we didn't get Locke's "right of revolution." The Americans did. The Canadians didn't.

The right of revolution entitles the American people to overthrow their constitution. In the day-to-day affairs of the nation, the legislature, executive, and courts act for the people in the name of "the people," but the people nevertheless retain the ultimate authority. They could abolish the presidency, Congress, and the courts. The whole applecart. How would it be done? The citizens might rise in armed revolt. Or they might take the peaceful route of establishing a national founding convention.

There's no comparable doctrine in Canada. That's the usual argument. Yet it's not easy to see what this way of thinking about the two nations adds up to. Americans haven't had any popular revolutions in the past one hundred and fifty years or so. They don't make even small amendments to their constitution very often. Indeed, American scholars today sometimes speak of the "absent sovereign." The suggestion seems to be that the American sovereign is like a sleeping giant. It might wake up. It's probably important to believe it could. But no one can image circumstances in which it will.

In contrast, Canadians in recent years have made major changes to their constitution. In 1982 we adopted a new Constitution Act, which contains the Canadian Charter of Rights and

Freedoms, an amending formula, and some other items including special guarantees for aboriginal peoples. We added the new act to the original British North America Act, and at the same time changed the name of the BNA Act, and some other constitutional statutes, as a signal that Canada was entering a new era. (The British North America Act, 1867 became the Constitution Act, 1867.) We also amended the Constitution Act, 1867. We passed the whole package by means of a rather clunky amending formula, one Peter Russell considers unsatisfactory. But pass it we did, with lots of noise, publicity, and bright lights, with the approval of the Canadian Supreme Court. And, if the poll data is correct, to great popular acclaim.

Then, fired by success, we drafted, and debated at length in public forums, in the legislatures, in the media, and over back fences two more ambitious constitutional documents. Powerful opposition elites killed the first one, the Meech Lake Accord. A national referendum killed the second, the Charlottetown Accord. But some people, some segments of the country, haven't given up hope that we'll try again. Changing Canada, changing our fundamental law, changing our goals and visions has become something of a national preoccupation. It's our "odyssey," as Peter Russell says. The Americans have had no comparable experiences recently. In their wildest dreams they don't entertain thoughts of such furious constitutional activity.

I think you could say the Canadian popular sovereign is up and about, stalking the land and shooting from the hip. But Canadian scholars continue to talk about the lively sense of popular sovereignty in the United States, and its absence in Canada! (Still lecturing from old notes!)

Prudent British, American, and even Canadian political thinkers have always been wary about appealing directly to the sovereign people on major constitutional issues. Insofar as it legitimates the right of revolution, careless talk about the popular sovereign may promote local riots and civil disobedience. Insofar as it depicts "the people" as a single collective entity, it can encourage democratic demagogues. If some one individual or group arises to give the giant a voice, that "one" may become the "single despot." So goes the liberal argument.

According to liberals, electoral and legislative politics are the better route to reform, even if they work only imperfectly. Better to let sleeping giants lie. Or nap. When all is going well the giant keeps one eye open, watching the political parties and leaders, lending support or withdrawing it, but refrains from using its full, wide-awake strength to declare the underlying constitution illegitimate.

Everything done by government and the courts is done in the giant's name (or one of its aliases – the people, the crown, the monarch, the constitution, leviathan). Government is nothing without the giant. But the giant itself, if we remember that it is the total of all individuals in the country, has many activities that at least partially escape the compass of government: art, religion, philosophy, family, business, philanthropy. Politics isn't everything for the giant.

POPULAR SOVEREIGNTY: THE PARLIAMENTARY OPTION

It will be clear now that I believe the doctrine of popular sovereignty and its corollary, the right of revolution, has underpinned politics in this country from 1867. Scholars like Russell who argue that popular sovereignty was ignored at Confederation don't give enough attention to the idea that ratification of constitutional documents by parliamentary resolution can be considered a legitimate expression of popular sovereignty.

Let's look at the Confederation arguments again. There's more to be learned. Both sides of the old quarrel show us features of parliamentary responsible government we have not yet explored. They show us especially why we must think of parliamentary responsible government as a form of liberal democracy.

Here's another formulation of the argument for ratification by parliamentary resolution alone. The contention is that a parliamentary majority has more legitimacy than a referendum majority because each "representative, though elected by one particular county, represents the whole country, and his legislative responsibility extends to the whole of the country." The speaker is Joseph Cauchon in the Canadian Legislative Assembly (1865). Cauchon touches briefly on the idea that there might be a tension between the member's responsibility to the "county," that is, to his riding, and to "country," the nation, but does not dwell on it. His chief point is that a member's responsibility for the "whole of the country" underpins Parliament's deliberative function. He says: "Our constitution is constructed upon the model of the British Constitution, and ... members do not and cannot receive an imperative order from their electors." The point is exactly Burke's in the famous *Address to the Electors of Bristol*. The member of Parliament sits for a particular constituency and must not neglect its interests and demands. But he (or today, of course, she) is also a participant in the grand process of arriving at measures in the national interest.

A delegate who was restricted to representation of constituency alone would not be free to deliberate, would not be free to change his or her mind in the face of superior arguments, indeed would not be free to change others' minds. The legislature's decisions would be arrived at by a process of declaring positions and counting. There would be no discussion, no argument, no mutual striving to reach the best verdict. There would be no deliberation.

Here is John A. Macdonald on parliamentary deliberation. Like Cauchon, he is opposing the referendum option. "Why, sir, for what do we come to this house, if it is not because we are supposed to be convinced by argument, if it is not that we are to sit down together and compare notes and discuss the questions that may come before us, and to be convinced according to the force of the reasons that may be advanced for or against them? And if we are honest, conscientious men, we change our opinions as we become convinced that that which we held before was wrong and the opposite right." Macdonald concludes that a referendum is objectionable because it would send instructed delegates into Parliament, that is, members unable to deliberate. This is the heart of his position. Since Parliament represents the entire people, a majority vote in Parliament is the fruit of structured deliberation based on respect for the political minority (the political opposition in the house and in the general populace). It is thus more inclusive and less authoritarian than the raw majority vote of a referendum. In my opinion Macdonald's argument is very strong. But ...

POPULAR SOVEREIGNTY: THE REFERENDUM OPTION

The referendum camp respects parliaments quite as much as the parliamentary camp. No less than their opponents, they believe that Parliament secures rights and promotes fruitful deliberation. Their question is this: What happens to the security for rights and to Parliament's power to deliberate when parliaments are "destroyed" by the act of founding?

They regarded the union proposal as a "revolution." They acknowledged that Confederation promised a new foundation for deliberation and rights. But that new foundation would be built on the ruins of the present one. The present foundation would be "swept away," "signed away." The new provincial governments would rise on a different footing and have different powers. Such a change of foundation, such a change in the security for rights – such a change in the social contract – required direct consultation.

William Annand says in the Nova Scotia House of Assembly (1866): "It was a matter of very serious import to the people of this province ... that their rights and privileges were to be swept away without their being consulted." George Sinclair says in the Prince Edward Island Assembly (1865): "What authority had the delegates [to the Quebec Conference] to go to Canada and thus sign away our rights." William Wetmore of New Brunswick argues that the Quebec delegates went "to Canada at great expense to the people of this country and there [matured] a scheme to destroy and sacrifice the country in which they live."

In the Canadian Legislative Council (1865), Benjamin Seymour puts the case this way: "Here you propose to change the constitution – to change the whole fabric of society – in fact to revolutionize society, without asking the consent of the people – at any rate, the reasonable possibility – of this important change ever being reconsidered." It is one of the great guarantees of political freedom in deliberative democracies – one of the guarantees associated with responsible government – that the electorate as agents of the sovereign people can turn out unpopular rulers and demand repeal of unpopular legislation. It is equally important that the electorate can change its mind again, return the original party, and even propose re-enactment of former laws. The term in constitutional law associated with this freedom is "parliamentary sovereignty." The electorate, the people, are not bound to respect and maintain statutes and policies enacted by previous governments. That's freedom. That's democracy.

When constitutional law is being made, this freedom is in

jeopardy. Constitutional law is the law for making statutes. It's sometimes called "superior" law. It's meant to "bridle democracy," to curtail oligarchy, and to shut up despots.

In the Nova Scotia House of Assembly (1866), Stewart Campbell argues that Confederation is a "matter which concerns [the people's] interests for all time to come." At present, he goes on, "if we have a ministry that is not agreeable to our wishes and that does not promote the interests of the country, we may bear with it for a while, knowing that the time will come when the people will assert their rights and substitute better men, but in reference to this measure only pass it now and it will be passed forever – the doom of Nova Scotia will then be sealed." In 1867 Nova Scotia's Archibald McLelan says: "Our system of government implies that you have either had the sanction of the people or intend to return to them for ratification. This bill does not contemplate that you should do that, for the very act destroys the constitution, and is contrary to the term – responsible government."

To approve Confederation was to take a step that could not be replicated and *could not be undone*. It could not be replicated because the institutions that had done the deed would have passed out of existence. The parliaments that had passed the resolution as part of the old order by their very act destroyed themselves. Thus, the people had to speak directly, in their own voice. A parliamentary resolution would not suffice. That's the heart of the case for consulting the people directly in a referendum.

And so we have the dilemma. The one camp says that a parliamentary resolution on Confederation will better protect the people's rights because Parliament is a deliberative arena. It will have more legitimacy than a referendum because more inclusive. The other camp argues that a parliamentary resolution on Confederation can have no legitimacy because the act of passing it destroys the Parliament and thus blows the supports out from under parliamentary rights and high-falutin' boasts about deliberation.

FAST FORWARD: HOW WAS IT DONE IN FACT?

It was clear to all that one way or another there would have to be legislative resolutions. The question was whether those resolutions would be passed by parliaments tied down by referendum results or by parliaments free to deliberate.

Most provinces found a halfway house. They held a general election in the expectation that the new Parliament would deliberate and bring the issue to a vote early in its term. In the Newfoundland general election of 1869, the people rejected the party favouring Confederation and the provincial elites accepted the verdict as final. The people had spoken. The Confederate leaders did not put the resolution to Parliament and Newfoundland did not come in.

British Columbia, New Brunswick, and Prince Edward Island held elections, voted in majorities for union, and passed the necessary resolutions. But in Nova Scotia there was no election prior to the parliamentary vote. Though the provincial Parliament approved union, the deed was done at the end of the parliamentary term, when it was far from clear that it had the support of the populace.

There was no election on Confederation in the province of Canada. In Canada, however, almost everyone in the two legislative houses was convinced from his own knowledge of his constituents that support for Confederation was high.

Red River is decidedly an exception. The Dominion of Canada more or less ignored the lively debate on Confederation in the councils of Red River and, in outright violation of the principle of popular sovereignty, simply annexed the population. In the Prince Edward Island House of Assembly (1870), Alexander Laird decried the unjust treatment of the Red River settlers: "[The] North-West Territory had been purchased, at a cost of £300,000 sterling What right ... had the people of the several provinces to pay this money for lands which should be the property of the settlers in that country? It was no wonder that the halfbreeds of Red River had rebelled against being literally sold, no wonder that the Honourable Joseph Howe should caution them to look after their own rights and inhabitants of the territory. Now was the time for them to see their lands ..."

Can we conclude that in most instances members of Parliament had taken steps to consult the people and were satisfied that, given practical circumstances, the people had consented? Yes. In most instances. We can certainly say that the exceptions left a bad taste. And we can say without fear of contradiction that both sides in the debate, those who were satisfied that parliamentary deliberation and resolutions would suffice, and those who insisted on direct consultation of the people, respected the Lockean idea that government is illegitimate without the people's consent.

REPRISE: RIGHTS AND DELIBERATION

"Both sides see parliament as the arena in which deliberation secures minority rights and promotes measures for the common good." Today we make heavy weather of assertions like this. At some point in our political history, perhaps not long ago, we lost confidence in the power of deliberation. As I write, newspapers are full of evidence. Feminists refuse to sit with men at a government-sponsored forum on the reform of family law. Canada's senior native leader threatens to organize a blockade of highways from coast to coast unless Ottawa abandons its planned overhaul of the Indian Act. International protestors struggle with police at summit meetings of world leaders. In most cases the activists claim to endorse democracy; they want more "transparency," more "inclusive" proceedings. They want to come "in" to the arenas of power. They want to be "heard." But we are a world away from the idea of participatory politics that prevailed in the Confederation period: civil, hopeful, eschewing violence, confident that reasoned debate among opposed positions is our best chance.

At some point we began to think of legislatures as a threat to rights, careless of our freedoms. We came to believe the courts are the better hope for securing liberties. And we began to think in terms of an opposition between the common good and individual rights. An either/or: either the common good *or* individual rights. According to this way of thinking, majorities flourish at the expense of minorities. Public safety requires restriction of legal rights, for example, the rights of the detained and the accused, the right to a fair trial.

No doubt there is at least some truth in the either/or. Majorities sometimes neglect minorities; who doubts it? But if we give this way of thinking too much credence, if we allow it to fill our minds entirely, it will take us far from the old confidence in political deliberation and parliamentary institutions. Insofar as we adopt the either/or exclusively, regard for Parliament, indeed regard for liberal democracy, goes by the boards.

The older idea said simply that security for rights and legislation for the common good are more likely in the liberal democracies. In the parliamentary and presidential democracies, rights and the common good flourish together.

THE COMMON GOOD

In the years after Confederation, the Conservative Party instituted a number of nation-building programs, referred to as the National Policy. Trade tariffs would protect the business interests of the eastern provinces from the machinations of the American economy to the south. Immigration policy would steer newcomers to the relatively unpopulated territories of the west to secure it against U.S. incursions. In other words, Macdonald and his colleagues had a political vision of the new Canada.

It is sometimes said about this visionary element in his make-up that it proves Macdonald was not a liberal, and certainly not a liberal democrat. The notion depends on the either/or I described above. Pure liberalism is supposedly concerned with individual rights. It's therefore reluctant to entertain visions of the national good. Macdonald's Conservatives must have inherited their willingness to consider the common good from the United Empire Loyalists or some other "red tory" source.

But parliamentary government has always allowed and encouraged the development of programs in the national interest and for the common good. Patrick Malcolmson argues that British parliamentary government has a strong bent towards the pragmatic. I agree. Parliamentary responsible government is an excellent machine for getting things done. It is also, as I have suggested, an excellent machine for contesting programs.

When we take into account the description of Parliament as a deliberative arena that promotes rights and enables legislation for the common good, do we have a sufficient picture of parliamentary government as liberal democracy? Will we be satisfied at last that the Fathers were liberal democrats? Perhaps. Nothing will satisfy the dyed-in-the-wool romantic democrat, whose heart will ever yearn for more emphatic expression of the will of the people. But we will have made the best case possible.

PART THREE
Bringing in the Future

10

Last Train from Right-Centre-Left

I said above that historians have trouble locating "democracy" and "equality" in our political history. The fact is that Canadian historians are relatively uninterested in political philosophy. They don't see it as their job to play around with ponderous and abstract notions like "democracy." And why should they? It's not their field.

Now recall the scholars of "right-centre-left." These are academics for whom philososophical abstractions are meat and drink: breakfast, lunch, and dinner. And as they tell it, Canada's history can't be understood except as a record of the progressive development of philosophical concepts. To understand Canadian Confederation one must know Locke and Rousseau, Montesquieu, Hegel, and Marx. Of course.

And yet, perhaps not surprisingly, the philosophers come to the same conclusion as the historians. Canada in 1867 wasn't a democracy. It may have been a liberal society, even a liberal democracy. But it wasn't a *true* democracy, a strong democracy. Indeed, so the argument goes, Canada still today is not a democracy.

THE PHILOSOPHERS OF RIGHT-CENTRE-LEFT

We must give our attention to the fact that right-centre-left makes a distinction between liberalism and liberal democracy. Liberal democracy is said to come after liberalism and before socialism. The complete continuum, as thinkers like Gad Horowitz describe it, is as follows: conservatism, liberalism, liberal democracy, and socialism.

Each stage supposedly generates the next; each historical era occasions political dissatisfactions that give rise to ideas about reform; the new ideas, translated into practice, create new dissatisfactions, which ... (Hegel's philosophy of history is the pattern; thesis generates antithesis; thesis and antithesis unite in synthesis; the synthesis then asserts itself as the new thesis, which generates its antithesis ... and so on. The world mind is a perpetual motion machine.)

In the version of this argument developed by Louis Hartz and Gad Horowitz to describe Canada, conservatism is said to be an ideology of "community" and "hierarchy" (collectivism and deference) with roots that go back to the feudal Middle Ages. Dissatisfaction with the experience of community and hierarchy generates the concepts of individualism and equalitarianism. Hence the liberal revolt of the seventeenth century. In 1688 the English adopt individualism and equalitarianism as foundational principles. But, though the idea of hierarchy is diminished by the developments of the seventeenth and eighteenth centuries, "community" retains its kick. For some reason, it doesn't die; it doesn't fade away. It goes underground. Or so Hartz and Horowitz suggest. "Community," so oppressive when experienced in the hierarchical relations of feudalism, lingers in the corners of history as a concept that might be independently worthy. And when the time comes, when history's ripe, "community" re-emerges to unite with liberalism in a new ideology, liberal democracy. (Imagine streams converging, or air currents colliding.) When does this convergence occur? Sometime in the mid-nineteenth century, say some thinkers. Not until the twentieth century say others. Estimates vary.

I have already suggested that some political scientists and philosophers see John A. Macdonald's National Policy as evidence that there was at least a "touch" of that lingering respect for community in British North America at the time of Confederation. Horowitz argues that this touch of conservatism was inherited from the American Tories who fled the revolution and came to British North America as the United Empire Loyalists. Thus, in the Confederation years, the elements for generating liberal democracy were present – supposedly: pre-democratic liberalism, as part of our British heritage from 1688, and the magic touch of collectivism, bequeathed us by the Loyalists. We had the ingredients! Or so it's said. But did we shake the cocktail? Were Macdonald's Conservatives indeed liberal democrats?

Horowitz says less on the development of liberal democracy than he might because he is not really interested in it. He is already looking forward to the kind of democracy enabled by socialism. We've seen that Justice Duff thought that the Dominion of Canada was a democracy from 1867. Duff, of course, didn't distinguish between "democracy" and "liberal democracy." In Duff's time, it was the accepted view that Canada from its founding was a parliamentary democracy. The new picture of the Canadian identity that gained credence in the 1960s suggested otherwise. We were probably liberals in 1867, whig liberals with a touch of toryism. We were bourgeois liberals, philistine liberals, but we may not have been liberal democrats. The Fathers of Confederation were hostile to true democracy and may have rejected liberal democracy. (So it's said.) Why weren't they true democrats? Why weren't they liberal democrats? Well, it was too early! The world, or Canada, had not matured sufficiently. Oh, the tyranny of right-centre-left!

FURTHER LESSON IN THE DIALECTIC

It's crucial to Horowitz's account of Canada that we received a touch of conservatism with the Loyalist immigration, and equally crucial that we received *only* a touch. The "touch" explains a good deal about us, according to Horowitz, not least the fact that Canada in the twentieth century, unlike the United States, generated socialist parties, like the CCF and its successor, the New Democratic Party. But Horowitz suggests that, because we received *only* a touch of conservatism, and have no vibrant national memories of feudalism, socialism remains a weak force.

The reader may ask how exactly ideas are transmitted from generation to generation. Should we be searching old archives, libraries, looking at legal texts? Do ideas cling to institutions in some fashion? What does it mean to suggest that ideas lodge in the mind of a nation? But dear friend, to ask this question takes you far off the track. Hartz and Horowitz are describing a process by which ideas generate further ideas. They describe a "dialectic." The human vehicles are incidental. Individuals don't "come up with" ideas. They give voice to them. Ideas rule.

Thus Horowitz has little need to study Canadian historical documents. He knows that the Loyalists must have been carrying that tory touch because if they hadn't been, Canadian socialism would not have arisen one hundred and fifty years later. He does not need to read the Loyalist writings. (And he doesn't.) Macdonald must have participated in that conservative Loyalist heritage because if he hadn't he wouldn't have drafted the National Policy. We have the dialectic's word: liberalism alone doesn't give rise to visions of the common good.

C.B. Macpherson is another who makes a distinction between liberalism and liberal democracy. In Macpherson's opinion, Locke was a liberal, but not a liberal democrat. None of the seventeenth- and eighteenth-century liberals was a liberal democrat. Liberal democracy emerged only slowly out of liberalism's contradictions, perhaps as early as Jeremy Bentham and James Mill in the first decades of the nineteenth century, but very probably not until later.

Let's think about what it means to say that Locke and the eighteenth-century thinkers were not liberal democrats. Among the principles and institutions Locke recommends, as we have seen, are the consent of the governed (tipping the hat to popular sovereignty), the right of revolution, the rule of law, equality under the law, representative parliaments, frequent elections, limited government, individual rights, and judicial independence. Locke is famous for opposing hierarchy. He argues resolutely against arbitrary and paternalistic government.

Macpherson's thesis, that Locke is not a liberal democrat, that Locke does not acknowledge democracy in any form, says, in effect, that the principles I have just listed, including the opposition to oligarchy, do not lie at the heart of democracy. Macpherson knows – indeed he does – that Locke stood for those principles. He knows that Locke opposed patriarchy and arbitrary government. He is saying that such opposition may be antithetical to the development of democracy. He is saying that liberalism is inherently anti-democratic. It can be brought into harness with democracy only with difficulty. The principles of liberalism do not necessarily benefit the *demos*, the people. So Macpherson's argument goes. Liberal principles are, perhaps, something like lies. They promise benefits but do not deliver. According to Macpherson's version of the dialectic, every form of government prior to socialism benefits only the "few." Liberalism and liberal democracy are no exception. They perpetuate the rule of the privileged few who belong to the capitalist class.

Remember that Hartz and Horowitz believe a dash of "community" helps to nudge liberalism in the direction of liberal democracy. Macpherson agrees. But, unlike Hartz and Horowitz, he doesn't waste time looking around for remnants of *feudal* thought on community. Though he acknowledges that history in early periods reveals pockets of what he calls "utopian" democracy (fantasies left over from ancient times, quaint Rousseaustic notions of the small agrarian community), in his opinion utopian democracy left no progeny. It has no real influence in the modern period; it has no place in the dialectic. Ideas have power only insofar as they are expressions of economic relations and class conflict.

Thus, Macpherson contends that liberal democracy develops only after the miseries of the industrial revolution have created a working class with at least a glimpse of its role in history. Bentham and James Mill record the development of this class but they perhaps fail to see its ramifications. They detect merely the glimmerings of liberal democracy.

The Moving Finger writes. The economic levers turn. Eventually we see true liberal democracy emerging, probably towards the end of the nineteenth century. And at some point after that come socialism and socialist democracy. The true democracy associated with socialism does not arrive everywhere at once. Writing in the 1960s and 1970s, Macpherson describes the Soviet Union as a sterling example of socialist democracy, one to be emulated. He had seen the future! He had hopes that an even more exemplary form of democracy was coming to life in the one-party political systems of post-colonial Africa. (Perhaps you hear the agitated liberal whispering: Evil Futures, Evil Futures. Stifle liberal sentiment for the time being.)

Macpherson didn't write about Canadian Confederation. But he had students. He had influence. He has undoubtedly made it easier for Canadian historians and political philosophers to argue that the Fathers of Canadian Confederation were not democrats and may not have been liberal democrats. And he certainly contributed to the idea, which we have already seen in Hartz and Horowitz (an idea still dear to romantics), that liberal democracy as it is found in the industrialized nations of the modern West is at best a second-rate regime. Liberal democracy is not true democracy.

Let me repeat: the distinction between liberalism and liberal democracy belongs to the particular school of thought found in Hartz-Horowitz and in Macpherson. It's widely taught in universities; it's set out at length in the textbooks. If we accept it, we're led to think that familiar features of liberal democracy, like the contestation of political parties, regular elections, and the rule of law are not sufficient for democracy, and indeed may even be incompatible with it. These familiar features of our system may be retarding us. If we were able to discard them, that is, to discard liberal democracy, we might advance to something finer.

That's the view from right-centre-left.

THE ONE-TWO PUNCH

Notice the double whammy.

First the historians (and some political scientists) suggest that there were few political ideas of importance in Canada's founding. Our founding legislators were severely lacking in philosophical endowment. Thus, there is no reason to think that they created institutions of enduring value.

Then come the philosophers. Whup! They assure us there *are* glorious ideas in Canadian history, ideas of great promise, carrying us along to a new day. But their version suggests even more emphatically that our *present* constitution is deficient. We are living with second-rate institutions.

It's hard to believe that constant repetition of these arguments has had no effect. Our present sense that individuals can't make a difference, our anger and apathy – the whole mixed bag of anxious feelings and arguments that surfaces in poll data and in surveys like those Keith Spicer conducted in 1991 may stem from our years in university classrooms.

CANADIAN POLITICAL HISTORY: REPRISE

Do I need to remind readers that the right-centre-left view of Canadian history promulgated by Horowitz and his followers is a fabrication? The great debates in British North America in the nineteenth century were not contests between feudal toryism and whig liberalism. They were about democracy. (Would the colonies adopt British parliamentary democracy in full measure, or work towards a more radical form, a more populist and romantic regime?) The men who enjoyed oligarchic power in the Family Compacts of the early nineteenth-century were not whiggish liberals touched by toryism whose feudal notions of noblesse oblige were gratefully accepted by a deferential populace. (As George Grant, for one, seems to suggest.) They were greedy men who took advantage of defects in the colonial constitution to grab power and hung on to it regardless of the popular will expressed in elections. They used their positions of power to do favours for family and friends. Theirs wasn't the worse regime in human history. Of course not. And they weren't despicable men. Many of them later, after the introduction of responsible government, became useful political leaders, converts to parliamentary democracy.

And Macdonald as we see him in the Confederation debates is not a feudal tory. Or tory-touched whig. He's a liberal democrat, somewhere in the mainstream. He argues for political deliberation, for the protection of minority rights, and for popular sovereignty (suitably represented by a parliamentary majority). He knew how to work with men of many political persuasions. In fact, he seems to have been a master in this area. He certainly knew the importance of including as many as possible from different persuasions in the process of constitution making. He knew the importance of making a constitution and regime that would allow the fullest possible expression of ideology and argument. It's wrong to suppose that Canada is the creation of the Conservative Party intended to benefit only Conservatives. Liberals (with a capital "L"), and indeed romantics – not a few – were among our nation builders.

There's no progression in our history from communal, deferential conservatism to individualistic liberalism, and then from individualistic liberalism to liberalism with a touch of democratic collectivity, and so on: from liberalism with a touch of collectivity to socialist collectivity. The parties that call themselves socialist come late in the story, it is true. But, as we shall see, there are socialists and socialists; some are firmly grounded in the political ideas of the Enlightenment and some have embarked on the seas of romanticism. The better structure for thinking of Canadian political history and Canadian politics today remains the great division of the modern era between the Enlightenment and Counter-Enlightenment.

As I suggested in this book's early chapters, we're not likely to stop thinking in terms of right, centre, and left. The labels will remain useful if only because they now have such resonance and are so familiar. But I hope we will stop thinking in terms of necessary historical progression; to think in terms of a necessary progression is to devalue everything before the socialist "end."

CHANGING AMERICAN OPINION

Right-centre-left never had much currency in the United States. Many Americans, especially those in academe, call their society liberal, meaning to say that the United States is founded on principles that derive from the political thought of John Locke and the Enlightenment. Many, though not all, are proud of that Lockean foundation. Of course, Americans sometimes use "liberal" to refer to parties and programs favouring big government, just as Canadians do. "Liberal" is a complicated term! Nevertheless, the idea persisted: the American union embodies Lockean principles. And yet here's a curious thing. A school of thought has now emerged in the United States to suggest that Lockean liberalism was not the only influence on the American founding and perhaps not the major one. Scholars of this persuasion now argue that, from earliest days, the constitution and American political thought show the impact of a communal philosophy, an anti-liberal, anti-individualist ideology. This is the philosophy of "civic republicanism" whose presence Peter Smith detects in Canada's early history. Republicanism in this definition, you'll remember, emphasizes civic participation, the sense of community, and public virtue.

How significant was its influence on the American founding and history? Scholars differ. Was Locke present as well? Most say yes; some say no. According to Keith Whittington, "scholars continue to find traces of republicanism in American thought long after the founding era, [though] few suppose the Constitution exclusively reflects republican ideals." But Michael Sandel, for one, believes that the civic republican ideology reigned supreme at the time of the founding, and remained dominant until the late nineteenth century. In his view, liberal individualism did not gain the upper hand until the twentieth century.

In short, it remains the case that few American scholars adhere to the Hartzian model of right-centre-left. They don't think in terms of a historical progression from feudal conservatism, to liberalism, liberal democracy, and then, perhaps, to socialism. The entire elaborate theory on which George Grant's disciples – scholars like Gad Horowitz – erected their comparison of Canada and the United States – the entire structure that supposedly proves Canada's superiority – was never universally accepted south of the border and is now open to challenge by new scholarship in both Canada and the United States.

That the new American research appeals to some Canadian thinkers I have already noted. Peter Smith uses it to examine the events in nineteenth-century British North America. Charles Taylor is attracted to the idea that anti-liberal but equalitarian modes of thought are part of our pre-Confederation heritage. Smith's work is informed by the researches of historians like J.G.A. Pocock and Bernard Bailyn. Taylor's thoughts are prompted by a reading of Michael Sandel, who in turn draws on Pocock.

It's time to shuffle out of our bunchy outfits once and for all. Right-centre-left is just too confining. It doesn't help us to understand the past, and it's hopeless as a predictor of the future. George Grant is right about one thing. Whatever lies ahead for North America, it's not socialism in the form Louis Hartz described. Or in the form predicted by C.B. Macpherson. Canada won't have to endure the socialism of the old Soviet Union. Or Albania. Or the post-colonial African states. There may be Evil Futures ahead, but not those ones. Right-centre-left is bad history and poor political science.

11

Romantic Ideas: George Grant

Is Macpherson a romantic? Is Horowitz?

In a sense we're not entitled to this question. Right-centre-left is supposedly a way of talking *about* ideologies. It is not itself an ideology. It's a model, or theory. One shouldn't compare a model of explanation to the thing being explained.

Let's do it anyway.

Both r-c-l and romanticism inculcate disdain for liberal democracy. Both encourage utopianism – and dissatisfaction with the status quo. Indeed r-c-l easily adapts itself to romantic postures. Socialists allow themselves to enjoy defeats; they conjure a future of endlessly crushing obstacles against which to struggle futilely. The notion is entirely romantic. Oh, the joys of losing! And sometimes, perhaps surprisingly, socialists entertain ideas of a life at the utter end of history, when the chains of the dialectic are loosened and we are free to live spontaneously and to fulfil individual desires in communities without oppressive communal norms. Marx allowed himself romantic visions of this kind.

But there are differences. Right-centre-left at its most rigorous – unlike romanticism – has decided ideas about what humans are meant to be and how they are meant to live. It has at its heart a "doctrine of human good." (The term is George Grant's.) It argues that socialism is the better or best way of life because it prescribes a regime that allows people to be what they are by nature supposed to be. "How they are supposed to be" is defined in various ways, but presumably it rules out obvious vices on the traditional list, like selfishness. In practice, socialism has used government powers ruthlessly in the attempt to root out selfishness. Romantic enthusiasm is put to the service of r-c-l absolutes.

Romanticism typically believes that we have to get beyond fixed ideas of "the human good," beyond norms, standards, and customs. People may adopt standards from time to time, and even live by them for long periods, but it should always be understood that standards can be redefined. There isn't any "good" that humans are *naturally* supposed to be, any permanently existing idea of the "good life" to which we should conform. When the world's going well, people will create their individual lives and the life of their democratic community according to the rules of freedom alone. Romantics don't subscribe to the idea that free humans might give reign to vices. (Or perhaps it would be better to say that they sometimes allow themselves to forget it.) Vices like selfishness. Or bullying. Romantics are inclined to argue that vices are the product of constraint. When we're free at last, we'll be good. Promise!

Because right-centre-left entertains ideas of "the good," we say it is "foundationalist." Romanticism is "anti-foundationalist." The two approaches can dance around each other; they can flirt. Yes, indeed. But romanticism is always pulling away in the direction of radical self-creation and self-determination.

WHERE ARE THE FRIENDS OF LIBERALISM?

Where are the scholarly friends of liberalism? you ask. Ask away! In the world of Canadian academe, there are very few who see it as their task to explore sympathetically and defend the institutions and philosophy of liberal democracy. Political scientists typically approach the study of the Canadian constitution and Parliament by listing its defects. A course in Canadian politics at the university level will focus on Parliament's deficiencies, the shortcomings of the Supreme Court, the failures of the criminal justice system, the necessity of reforming the electoral system, the possibility of redrafting the division of legislative powers. Dilemmas, problems, crises! More theoretically inclined scholars throw their energies into elaboration of arguments for thinking liberalism's foundations imperfect. They criticize not only particular institutions and practices but the very idea of liberalism. The malaise of modernity! In short, the academic friends of liberalism are conspicuous by their absence. The critics are legion.

The book-jacket advertisement for Ronald Beiner's *What's the Matter with Liberalism?* reads as follows: "In the wake of the [European] revolutions of 1989 ... and the democratization of most of Latin America, what is the task of political theorists? Should they emphasize the theoretical strengths of liberal society, thus helping to consolidate the political gains recently experienced in the face of threatening regimes? Or should they challenge, probe, and explore with a skeptical eye the reigning assumptions of the [liberal] political community?" Beiner chooses not to emphasize the strengths of liberal society, as I hardly need to say. He takes on "the shibboleths of modern Western discourse"; he probes the "sterility of liberalism" and explores the "aridity of liberal societies." Beiner describes himself as a man who refuses to serve as "a source of ideological reassurance about our own superiority." He is searching for a political system that promotes "a more ethical and principled life" than liberalism allows. He envisions "some variant of socialism that promotes citizens' participation" and looks to the Socratic tradition for guidance. "Permitting ethos to replace values, and discourse about 'the good' to replace talk about 'rights,' enables the theorist to reorder social priorities." One has some sympathy. I want merely to note the romantic tone of the argument: it's always some other regime, some other place, some other era in human history that offers the superior remedy. The grass is always greener on the other side of the fence.

We have not yet seen the full range of arguments against liberal democracy in the romantic camp. In the next section we begin with George Grant.

GRANT'S LAMENT

Am I classifying George Grant as a romantic? A chorus of voices will rise to object, and with good reason. Among Canadian philosophers, Grant is the arch-foundationalist. He emphatically rejects the idea that freedom requires us to disregard notions of "the good for man." He believes we become free by living the life God intends for us. He has a soft spot for the Marxists exactly because they retain an idea of "the human good," "the good for man." No, the teaching I associate with the romantics, that humans must free themselves from limits imposed by history, belief, and custom to adopt ever new definitions of themselves and their community: this idea Grant opposes with every fibre of his moral being.

And yet I am convinced that all his writings have contributed to the growth of romanticism. He supremely promotes discontent with Canadian liberal democracy. He praises caution and prudence, but does it in a way that has made Canadians incautious and imprudent. He is an anti-utopian, but his words encourage utopianism.

His most famous book, *Lament for a Nation*, ends with a quotation from Virgil's *Aeneid: "Tendebantque manus ripae ulterioris amore."* "They were holding their arms outstretched in love toward the further shore." And what is that "further shore"? Is it the land of the living? (In the poem the inhabitants of the underworld "hold their arms outstretched in love" as they watch Aeneus take the upward path.) Is it the kingdom of God? Grant does not say. But countless readers have had no doubt that it is the New Canada. And that we must love and create it together. *Lament* is subtitled,*"The Defeat of Canadian Nationalism."* The irony is that so many have interpreted it to mean that Canadian nationalism can and must be made anew. To see how the archfoundationalist becomes the beloved of romantic anti-foundationalism we must first look at Grant and then at his interpreters.

At first reading, Grant seems to say nothing about the ideology I am calling romanticism. He certainly says little about Jean-Jacques Rousseau. I remember the day at McMaster University when the word went around that Grant at last was going to give a public lecture on Rousseau. The room was packed; there were students hanging in the open doors. (But what he said on that occasion was curiously unfocused.)

The fact is that Grant *does* write about romanticism – under another name. What I have been calling romanticism, Grant identifies as "liberalism," meaning by this not the liberalism of John Locke but a present-day development. It is an ideology he despises. He professes at least some respect for Lockean liberalism in original form, but argues that it has turned itself into, or has given rise to, a despicable philosophy of extreme freedom and human self-creation.

We must imagine ourselves once again in the world of the dialectic in which ideas generate ideas and doctrines transform themselves into their antithesis. Grant begins, just as Hartz, Horowitz, and Macpherson do, with the suggestion that Lockean liberalism arises from the struggle against conservatism. But he does not go on as they do to argue that liberal democracy and socialism follow in due course. Grant doesn't see socialism as the end of world history.

The clue lies in his understanding of conservatism. For Grant, conservatism is supremely the way of thinking about politics that legitimates the restriction of human freedom in the name of "the human good." It is a definition that is compatible, at least in bare outline, with the feudal ideology that right-centre-left depicts as a combination of hierarchy and collectivism. But right-centre-left, you will remember, admires only the collectivist element in this conservative ideology. Grant, in contrast, admires both the collectivism and the hierarchy. He admires the collectivist component because, to put it simply, he is a nationalist. As a philosopher, he prefers particularity and nationality to what, following Leo Strauss and Alexandre Kojève, he calls "the universal and homogeneous state." In other words, he likes national traditions, local communities, and family traditions. He rejects the idea of world citizenship, or allegiance to vague universal notions of justice, as both impossible and, in some fundamental sense, inhuman.

He admires the hierarchical element in conservatism because it is "good in itself" and also because it is necessarily a feature of a political society built on the idea of the good for man. Hierarchy goes hand in hand with the requirement that politics conform to a communal idea of the good. In a political society defined by the good, only some individuals, only the "few," will measure up, and – so goes the argument – they are the ones entitled to govern. They are the ones whose rule will be accepted as legitimate. Grant desires communal expression of the good for man as a necessary restriction on human freedom, and so he welcomes hierarchical rule.

In Grant's version of the dialectic, liberalism, struggling against its predecessor in the manner of ideologies, casts off all idea, conservative or indeed socialist, that there are natural or God-given restraints. In its original form, Lockean liberalism had prescribed at least minimal restraints. But these restraints were perhaps insufficiently grounded; at any rate, in the campaign against the absolute rulers of the seventeenth century (the Stuarts, the Bourbons), they lost legitimacy. Thus, Lockean liberalism survives today only "on the periphery" of politics. So Grant argues in *Lament*. Lockean liberalism is a "museum piece." In Canada and in North America today, the dominant ideology is a liberalism that encourages us to create and recreate ourselves and our communities in the belief that endless possibilities of enterprise and conquest lie before us. And in Grant's opinion – here is the heart of his contention – such an ideology opens the door to the boundless expression of human vice. When humans believe they can, indeed must, transcend or transform all moral and political constraints, they can do terrible things to themselves, to each other, and to their world.

The argument is powerful. And if we accept it, we will have to admit there's no distinction of the kind I have been trying to make between liberalism as we know it today and romanticism. There's only one ideology abroad now – call it liberalism, call it romanticism – and it is delivering us to evil. The Enlightenment doctrine of the seventeenth and eighteenth centuries, which its progenitors so confidently expected to bring in an age of universal peace and human dignity, declined "ineluctably" (a favourite word of Grant's), declined inevitably, into the philosophy that produced the Evil Futures of the twentieth century. And worse is to come.

Rather than take on an argument of such magnitude, I propose that we adopt an easier route and look at Grant on Canada. Grant isn't the only critic of modernity. His importance for us, I suggest, is that he makes the case in terms of Canadian history and experience.

When we shift our focus to Canadian history and Canada today, Grant's argument begins to fray around the edges. I have already suggested that it's built on a poor understanding of history; it doesn't describe the facts of political life in British North America. Like Hartz and Horowitz, Grant accepts the idea that the United Empire Loyalists endorsed collectivism and hierarchy; that is, he supposes their political thinking was marked by at least a "touch" of feudal conservatism. He regards the colonial oligarchies, the Family Compacts, as bearers of this salutary conservatism with its teaching about necessary restraints. Better oligarchy under God-fearing men (and women, no doubt) than the liberation of the passions prescribed by degenerate liberalism, because the liberation of the passions will surely deliver us into the cruel hands of amoral elites.

(I hope your mouth is hanging open. Grant isn't rejecting liberal democracy in the name of something *more* democratic, in the manner of Horowitz and Macpherson. He wants something less democratic. He's defending oligarchy. How far is he prepared to go? Does he endorse the divine right of kings, or the rule of a priestly class? And what *about* democracy? What about equalitarianism? What about human rights?)

I've said before that there's little in the documents to suggest that the Loyalists were conservatives in Grant's sense. Many were Lockean liberals. Some at least tell us that they fled to Canada because they thought their individual rights would be better protected under British rule than under American republicanism. But they were not a homogeneous lot. Peter J. Smith believes that many were what he calls "civic republicans" who argued for equalitarian and virtuous communities. Some, perhaps many, seem to have admired the governments they were leaving behind. As Kenneth McRae notes, a dozen reasons lie behind the Loyalist exodus. He believes that most were liberals. He writes, "In Canada we encounter once again the American liberal." The one thing we can assert with confidence is that, liberal or republican, they did not entertain a markedly hierarchical philosophy. Neither Lockean liberalism nor civic republicanism accepts institutionalised hierarchy. The Loyalists were equalitarians, no doubt imperfect ones, but equalitarians just the same.

Grant was right to argue that many of the Loyalists were religious men and women. Religious belief was not unusual in the nineteenth century. (It's not unusual today.) But here is a peculiar thing. Grant supposes that liberalism (Lockean or "romantic") requires secularism. But does it?

Let me suggest that, unless the state encroaches on freedom of religion in overt fashion, religious men and women in liberal democracies manage in some fashion or another to engage in fruitful political dialogue with non-believers, to the advantage of all. It may be, as Kant says, that liberal democracy can be run by a race of intelligent devils. But theists can also run it. And if the institutions are well set up and respected, theists and "devils" rub along. In a liberal democracy no one is, no one should be, excluded on the basis of belief or non-belief in the deity. (On this subject vast avenues of thought beckon. Philosophers devote their lives to it.) I will merely say that one is not required to give up belief in God to live in a liberal democracy. In the political arena, arguments originating in religious belief are not favoured over others; neither are they automatically excluded.

The trouble in the British North American colonies in the early nineteenth century was not that some colonists were believers and some were not (or that some were Loyalists and some rebels, or even that some were romantics and some were liberals). The trouble was that the imperial connection enabled a few colonists – the oligarchic cliques – to grab and hang on to power without effective political challenge.

THE LOVER

As a teacher, George Grant is surely remembered for his lectures on love. Whatever the assigned text, classroom discussions would come back to questions of friendship, patriotism, the love of "one's own," the love of "the good," love for God. How often, with what ardour, we explored the seeming opposition between love of one's own and love of the good. The love of one's own – personal and private passions, family and tribal affiliations: Does such love lead one by stages to the love of the good absolutely, as Socrates seems to say in *The Symposium*? Does the comparison of particular loves and "goods" bring one at last to The Good? Yet Grant often said that the idea of The Good, and the great abstractions that are aspects of it – Truth, Beauty, Humanity – never have the fierce hold on our hearts that our particular loves have. Only the saints love Humanity with the passion of parents for children. So the discussions went.

As a writer he will be remembered for teaching us to love Canada. Like Horowitz, he shows us Canada in the context of great political and philosophical ideas in human history. Even today, re-reading *Lament for a Nation*, I feel the old enchantment beginning to work. I believe the book will stay in print for as long as the country endures. It appeals because of the sheer sweep and boldness of the argument. And because it speaks to deep emotions. Do Canadians in English Canada love their country? I remember the reaction of a student who watched Quebec lose the provincial referendum on sovereignty. Seeing Jacques Parizeau's tears in the close-ups, he understood that the man had lost more, much more, than a referendum or election. The emotion of that evening went far beyond the usual excitement of election night. Parizeau had lost a country. And my student was consumed by jealousy. He knew then that he had in his own public life as an English-speaking Canadian no sentiment, no attachment, of comparable depth. And he wanted it.

Yes, Grant aroused our passion for Canada. He promised us a truly loveable Canada. And yet the nation he describes is not immediately recognizable. It does not appear to include the provinces of the west, for example. The early chapters of *Lament* tell the story of one westerner, the Conservative Prime Minister John Diefenbaker. But it is impossible to escape the conclusion that the work as a whole centres on the "heartland," Ontario and Quebec, with an occasional glance at the Maritimes. Moreover, the Quebec it describes is the Quebec of the years before the Quiet Revolution. Grant knew and understood what was happening in Quebec as the provincial Liberal Party and the Parti Québécois transformed the political society. But he did not approve. He did not love the new Quebec. And, for that matter, he did not he love the Ontario he saw coming into being in the 1960s. Or the new Canada. The country he loves is the Canada of his own youth.

Or is it? In my opinion it is a country almost entirely fabricated from his imagination and his personal preferences. The Canada Grant teaches us to love and lament never existed. It is a romantic fiction.

His great legacy comes down to this. He told Canadians, and many believed him, that the days of parliamentary liberalism are over, and that the "liberal" philosophy now dominating our politics is at best deficient, and more probably dangerous. Dangerous to our national identity and to our moral health. He told us, and many believed him, that in the eternal order of things Canada is a conservative country. That crucial touch of conservatism was our inheritance. It defined our identity. But we are losing it. It is already lost. "The impossibility of conservatism in our era is

Romantic Ideas: George Grant

the impossibility of Canada." This is the most famous sentence in *Lament*. Grant taught us that Canada was impossible. He taught us to disdain liberal democracy and he offered nothing in its place.

Can we now see why he must be described as a romantic? To mourn for the irretrievable past is the very stuff of romantic poetry, the romantic high arts, and, for some nations, political identity. Right-centre-left may keep its eyes resolutely on the future. Liberalism may confidently hope for better days. But romanticism dawdles, looking over its shoulder at golden ages past. It glories in nostalgia, in the delicious idea that one has been deprived, that one suffers. As Tom Lehrer tells us, "the losers have all the good songs." Yes, Grant, despite his foundationalism, is a romantic. The deep pessimism, the idea that the great tides of history are sweeping us towards an inescapable Evil Future – this is romanticism! His picture of that Future as a dreary round of consumerism and pettiness in an environment degraded by the greed and ambition of industrialists – romanticism!

But who would have believed that Canadians would adopt this self-pitying line of thought? We're a successful and admired political society. We have one of the world's oldest political constitutions. We strive for justice, for the good of all citizens. We've won all our wars for the past one hundred and fifty years or so. People are clamouring to come here.

We're not losers.

GRANT'S FOUNDATIONALISM: REPRISE

The anti-foundationalist romantics rage against the constraints of nature, history, and law. Life gains meaning and purpose only when the artist is free to determine his own course and express his own "values." But – this is the overriding theme of some late romantics especially – the struggle against constraints is in vain. Nature, history, vile bourgeois society inevitably triumph, destroying art, crushing freedom, and thwarting self-assertion. Hence romantic despair.

As I have said, Grant believes that constraints reveal life's meaning. If our lives today seem purposeless, it is because we persist in trying to throw off limits ordained by nature, history, and law. We take as impediments to our flourishing the instructions that God has laid down for us. Hence Grant's despair. There are indeed profound differences between Grant and the romantics.

But the similarities cannot be denied: the Evil Future draws near. Dreary totalitarianism beckons. If we were to study particular romantics, we would find still more parallels. Grant's rejection of technology, his distrust of modern science, his profound anti-capitalism, his disdain for the pleasures of the mass age, his savage scorn for things American: all have their echo in the work of one romantic or another. As Judith Shklar says: "Horror at technology and hatred of the masses are ... part of the romantic's estrangement in a 'totalitarian world.'"

The romantic feature of his writings that concerns us most is his contention that our age, our present situation, our constitution, are not worth our loyalty. We were meant to be otherwise. We've lost a precious possession.

THE INTERPRETERS

It's time for the second act. (It's short.) We must look at Grant's interpreters. They're mainly from right-centre-left and we have already met the chief among them, Gad Horowitz. Others are found in the school of thought known as "economic nationalism." It flourished in the 1960s and 1970s, and its legacy lingers.

The argument is that, though conservatism is impossible today, the essence of conservatism, its idea of collectivism, can still be fanned to life. A new Canada can be built on this new collectivism and it will preserve the essential, defining features of the old nation. Grant's suggestion that a collectivist philosophy entails elitism and hierarchy is abandoned. His description of Evil Futures is rejected. We're left with the idea that Canadian "collectivism" will be entirely pleasant, compatible with equalitarianism, caring, and tolerance. It's supposedly this community-minded doctrine about caring that distinguishes us today from the United States.

It is unfortunate that Grant's thought encourages crude and sometimes virulent anti-Americanism. The United States is depicted as a regime unable to rid itself of the baleful influence of liberal capitalism, suffering from an excess of egalitarianism that destroys everything fine and from an excess of individualism that promotes greedy, uncaring, insensitivity to the common good. It saddens me that such pettiness mars Grant's thought and it saddens me that anti-Americanism has come to loom so large in some Canadians' definition of themselves.

The facts don't support the conclusion. The United States spends more per capita on social welfare than does Canada. So much for our quality of caring! Individual Americans give more than individual Canadians to charity. And as for the idea that we're more tolerant, phooey! A glance at their national debates in Congress, a glance at their national newspapers and journals shows that the United States entertains a broader range of political ideas than does Canada.

Louis Hartz argued that, because the United States was settled in the era of liberalism, and thus inherited no significant conservatism (and, it follows, no socialism), political debate in that country is never anything more than a quarrel among liberals. Right-wing liberals quarrel with left-wing liberals. That's politics in the United States, according to Hartz. It lacks the richness and scope of political debate in Europe. Drawing on the same analysis, Gad Horowitz suggests that, because Canada inherited a modicum of conservatism (as he supposes), a "touch," it *must* be that debate in Canada spans a broader range than debate in the United States. We may not have Europe's exciting fascist and communist parties, but we can congratulate ourselves at least on having a political scene that's livelier than the scene in the States. But dear friends, political debate in Canada isn't broader. Certainly in the Canadian heartland, debate is narrower, nastier, and quite intolerant of departures from the Canadian middle of the road.

I suggested in Chapter 1 that Canadians are quite surprisingly hampered in their debate on social policies. We're buttoned up. We can't shed the draggy overcoat. We're hampered because the notion that we are in some hard-to-define way more caring than the United States requires us to favour welfarism. We can't think openly and freely on issues of the positive state. To entertain arguments against the positive state is to cast doubt on our credentials as a citizens of that mythic Canada beloved of Grant and his disciples.

For years, Canadians clung to a version of the argument about Canadian broad-mindedness, which said that Canada makes room for a wide variety of ethnic and cultural identities while the United States intolerantly insists that newcomers assimilate to the American way of life. Canada was said to be a "mosaic" of cultures (and therefore admirable). The United States was a "melting pot" (and therefore not admirable). The idea still lingers. But there's no evidence for it.

Both countries have welcomed immigrants and refugees. Both have accorded newcomers all the rights and freedoms of citizenship. There's no two-tier citizenship in Canada or the United States. Some newcomers retain their original languages, cultures, and religions while also becoming proficient in their new country's official language, or languages. They set up day schools or after-hours schools, community centres, and newspapers to support their particularity, sometimes with the assistance of public funds. At the same, time they move into the mainstream of public life. They open businesses, vote, run for public office, take advantage of public benefits. The pattern has been more or less the same in both countries. There are differences and I do not want to suggest that we ignore the differences entirely. I do argue that the similarities are more striking. Some newcomers jettison their original heritage. Some jettison it and then return to it. Or find to their amazement that their children are taking up professorships in the language of their parents' country of origin, or are moving back to their parents' religious beliefs.

Have there been injustices, failures? Yes. Human practices are always flawed. But on the whole both countries have felt compelled to try to live up to the equalitarian premises of liberal democracy and to the promise of popular sovereignty.

But there is one way in which Canada obviously differs. Because we need to see ourselves as unlike the United States, we're not as free to debate issues of immigration and citizenship. (The bunchy overcoat again!) We can't allow ourselves to think clearly about "assimilation" and "tolerance" because we are not supposed to be an assimilatory society like the intolerant United States. Thus, we can't ask what's intolerant about offering equal citizenship to immigrants in the manner of the United States. We can't ask what's intolerant about opening access to public funds and benefits, and inviting newcomers to participate fully in the economic and political life of the nation. We continue to think, in buttoned-up fashion, that the American offer of equal citizenship must be intolerant because it is destructive of particular cultures, while our very similar offer is tolerant because supportive of particularity. Confusion reigns.

We can't think clearly about our liberal-democratic heritage. We feel compelled to criticize its principles but can't see what's to replace them. We have vaulting ambitions and are convinced the country is failing. We want to grasp the future, retrieve the past, "to seek, to strive, to find, and not to yield." But how? How? Anger and apathy colour our public debates.

Am I blaming George Grant for all our discontents? No. But he and his interpreters have contributed.

12

Romance in a Democratic Clime

Grant's disciples encouraged anti-Americanism and left us with a confused sense that we ought to be throwing up barriers against the world. A certain confusion, a certain nastiness, impatience with liberal democracy: that's the legacy of the economic nationalists. But even as they were writing, other developments were coming to the fore in Canada and the United States.

THE NATIONALISM OF THE ROSE

One can't talk about nationalism in this country without at least a brief reference to Pierre Elliott Trudeau. Many Canadians, in English Canada at any rate, think of him as a latter-day Father of Confederation, the man who remade our constitution and gave us the nation we know today. His name is indelibly associated with the 1982 Canadian Charter of Rights and Freedoms (arguably now the greatest symbol of Canadian nationhood) and with "patriation," the constitutional reform that introduced a made-in-Canada amending formula, thus freeing us from the last vestiges of dependence on the Parliament of Great Britain.

A latter-day Father. Author of a nation. Was he a nationalist? He had a vision of Canada, undoubtedly. And he was willing to impose that vision in law. He was a master of the scholarly literature on nationalism. He wrote important essays on it. But did he truly understand it? It could be argued that, to understand the phenomenon we call nationalism, requires at least a shred of sympathy for the romantic perspective. And Trudeau had none.

He was, through and through, a liberal – a constitutionalist and foundationalist, perhaps a socialist (but if a socialist, a steely-hearted one). He did not understand sentimental cravings and behaviours, and certainly had no patience with them. He wore the costume of an old-fashioned romantic: think of the capes, slouch hats, and roses. He had panache and dash. Many loved him, and he loved being loved. But he was not a political romantic.

In the 1960s Trudeau published two essays to show that nationalism is an anomaly in today's world. He considered it something of an outrage that nationalism had arisen in modernity shortly after the birth of liberalism. In the rational world of the eighteenth century, where the heirs of the Enlightenment were purposefully working out their destinies in ways that would advance progress, democracy, peace, and justice, the nonsense of nationalism, patriarchy, and ethnicity *ought to have disappeared*. Such sentiments are barbarous. They serve no purpose. They can be dangerous. Democracy requires rational deliberation and rational deliberation is not compatible with mindless comittment. The combination, liberalism and nationalism, should not have happened. Ostensibly, Trudeau's essays are intended to explain nationalism's puzzling persistence. But they do not explain. They merely reveal the author's profound impatience with the phenomenon.

Consider his treatment of Quebec. To curtail Quebec's pretensions to separate nationhood, Trudeau included in the 1982 Charter of Rights and Freedoms clauses on the use of French and on access to education in French that directly challenged laws passed by the Quebec provincial legislature. He intended the Supreme Court of Canada to use the new Charter to strike down the provincial laws, and in due course the justices obliged. But did the demise (or to be more accurate, the impairment) of their language laws put an end to Quebec's desire for separate nationhood? Of course not! Being kicked in the teeth encourages nationalism. Glorious resentment and self-assertion surge to life! Anyone but a dyed-in-the-wool Enlightenment man like Trudeau would have known that.

Do we learn *anything* about nationalism from Trudeau? The sort of satisfaction Canadians have when they think about patriation and the Charter of Rights and Freedoms is sometimes called civic nationalism – as opposed to the full-blown romantic thing. Trudeau gave us civic nationalism and his writings suggest that he understood and had no objection to national feeling in this mild form. He regarded it indeed as salutary. A little *talk* about community and national goals? Why not? A little indulgence in national pride? Symbols? Charters? It's permitted. And most Canadians in English Canada find this civic nationalism sufficient.

Still, there's a curious thing about the Charter. We (in English Canada, at any rate) see it as a national document, an assertion of our national identity. And why shouldn't we? Nevertheless, it's Americanized us. Many of its clauses are more or less identical to clauses in the American Bill of Rights. I don't mean to say that the framers of the Canadian Charter copied the American document (though we know they had an eye on it). Rather they were drawing on the long tradition of legal rights that is found in English common law and that also influenced the American Founders more than two hundred years ago. But there it is. On paper we now look more like our neighbour. And, given the Charter, the Canadian Supreme Court now behaves more like the American Supreme Court. And Canadians, relying on the Charter, have become more prone to litigate constitutional and political issues – in this respect again imitating Americans. Our political culture is now less distinctive – because of the Charter.

Right on the heels of the economic nationalists, with their insistence that we recapture – or, add a pinch of romanticism here, *create* – a distinctive Canadian society and culture, came Trudeau with a pack of constitutional reforms, chief among them a constitutional bill of rights. We welcomed his reforms as a symbol of our identity. And they had the effect of diminishing our distinctiveness!

ROMANTIC NATIONALISTS

Romantic nationalists! One thinks of passionate assertions about the collective life and will, about the bonds of language, soil, race, and blood. Surely we don't have nationalists of that kind in Canada.

No indeed.

And yet, as Trudeau knew, something like it – echoes of it, the threat of it – runs through our history like fire. Remember the colonial oligarchies with their assertion of British superiority. Remember Catholic-Protestant riots in the Maritimes in the pre-Confederation years, anti-French sentiments in the new Dominion, and discrimination against black communities, against Jews, disdain for immigrants from Eastern Europe, the ill treatment of Asians.

To list our transgressions is to weep. There are also the hostilities that immigrants bring: the Mafia preyed on the Italian community; Tamils prey on their own in Toronto. Sentiments and cruelties like these are perennial. It's not surprising to find them surfacing in our history. Hence the liberal argument: to allow in public life anything stronger than civic nationalism invites assertions of superiority and inferiority. It invites injustice, hierarchy, gang wars, domestic terrorism. Sedition, conquest, death. The Evil Futures. But that's the liberal argument. What does the romantic say?

Canada's romantic nationalists don't appeal to blood and soil. They sometimes mumble about the bonds of language. But – this is surprising – on the whole they say little about Canada's distinguishing traits. They don't, for example, dwell on ways we differ from the United States. (They depart from right-left-centre in this respect.) No, today's romantics on the subject of Canada tend to sound just one note. They have one big thing to say. And this one big thing is that life in Canada is inherently unsatisfying. Life in all liberal democracies is unsatisfying and most certainly life in Canada is "arid" and "sterile."

You may say that this is a curious argument for nationalists. Don't nationalists praise their country? No, not if they're Canadian nationalists of a romantic bent writing today. They praise the idea of nationalism but they don't praise the nation. The argument is highly abstract and runs something like this. We're deficient because we don't value nationhood and don't encourage our national culture and because our cultural minorities can't fully express the characteristics of their particular heritages. To make this argument, you understand, nothing needs to be said to describe Canadian nationhood or the minority cultures. The contention is that cultural identity is valuable in and of itself, regardless of its content, so to speak.

But why is cultural identity valuable? In the last chapter I suggested that the various ethnic and religious groups in Canada (and in the United States) find ways to participate in the public life of the nation while still educating their children in their particular traditions and languages. I argued that, insofar as conflicts arise between national loyalties and loyalty to one's smaller community, individuals and families sort out the matter for themselves, sometimes choosing full participation in national affairs and sometimes immersing themselves in enclaves of their smaller associations. To the romantic, statements like this appear simplistic to the point of stupidity, showing deep ignorance of the human persona and human cravings.

This romantic argument goes beyond Grant's claim that individuals naturally love "their own," that is, desire association with a particular community. It contends rather that, in the absence of community, a person's individual identity is imperilled. A person knows herself as a person, as an individual, insofar as she sees her actions and attitudes reflected in the actions and attitudes of others in a community. Thus – to repeat – the problem isn't merely that one's life is poorer without a communal affiliation. (But one soldiers on, perhaps!) It's that one's sense of self, one's very capacity to live, to love, to soldier on, is threatened.

Hence the charge that life in liberal democracies is arid and sterile. We're missing something vital and we don't even know what it is! Liberalism's famous boast that the state treats all equally under the law, without regard to race, origin, or creed, requires that the individual check at the door of public life everything that makes him or her a fully realized person. Liberalism indeed admits only thin wraiths – bare, shivering selves. The liberal state makes light of the essential human need to be recognized as an individual *in all one's cultural complexity*.

The contention is often framed as an argument against the liberal philosopher John Rawls. To illustrate his definition of liberal justice, Rawls asks readers to imagine themselves in what he calls "the original position." You are standing outside life (perhaps about to enter!). You are intelligent and have power of choice but do not know whether in your (new) life you will be male or female, healthy or impaired, born to rich parents or poor, black or white, and so on. Now, says Rawls, while in this original position, imagine that you must choose the form of government that will give you the best chance for a good life. The form of government that gives the intelligent but ignorant chooser the best chance, he calls "just." Justice is what the naked self would choose from the original position. Liberals admire Rawls's imaginative exercise because it seems to prove, insofar as such exercises prove anything, the injustice of oligarchy, patriarchy, and so on. The chooser in the original position would be ill advised to opt for oligarchy! The odds for a good life would be poor indeed.

The romantic finds the exercise disturbingly wrongheaded. It's wrong, it's absurd, to imagine a being outside history and community – an "unsituated" self. Such an entity would not be human. Rawls is asking us to think of our essential selves as inhuman! More than this, he encourages us to define justice as the best regime for these inhuman beings. He wants a definition of justice that transcends time and place. But there can be no timeless justice, no universal justice, any more than there can be unsituated selves.

The romantic nationalist argues (insofar as he stirs himself to make concrete political proposals) that states must acknowledge the individual's "situated" character. To put it plainly, romantics want at the least a richer public life in which a person's aboriginality, or Jewishness, or Italian ancestry, or East European identity is recognized in law. They also want to see minority associations recognized. If a community is to offer adequate support for the development of individual identities, it must itself stand well with other communities and with the larger nation. Individuals require communal recognition, and communities require state recognition. Think of a rich, glowing cultural mosaic. In brief, the liberal state's refusal to assign political significance to race, ethnic origin, colour, or religious creed intolerably impoverishes citizens and denies them the affirmation that promotes the sense of political efficacy. Liberal blindness to race and other such cultural identifiers is positively undemocratic!

From the romantic perspective, Trudeau's policy of multiculturalism was promising but ultimately inadequate. It offered ethnic groups funding for cultural projects and recognition in the form of words, testimonials, scraps of paper. Romantics argue that cultural differences must be recognized in more permanent form – in the Criminal Code, and in justiciable clauses in the constitution. And, of course, in our hearts.

The teaching strikes a blow at the deep core of the Enlightenment. Liberals used to say that theirs was a fighting creed. Now it's embattled. Liberals stood – still do – for the universal brotherhood of man (or, as we should say, the kinship of women and men in every time and clime). They believe that justice truly defined is something applicable regardless of culture. They recognize, of course, that different nations and communities have different customs and different practices. Variety is the spice of life. Yet they insist that the underlying principles of good government are the same everywhere. Thus, they argue for international rights and freedoms, for programs to promote security, and for political education and political freedom for all persons in all countries. They don't agree about the means to secure these good things. (Liberals, as I've said often, believe that disagreement about means is inevitable – and salutary. Liberal democracy welcomes dissent.) Nevertheless, they agree that everyone should have these goods and that it should be the objective of the nations that enjoy them to do what they can to spread them throughout the world.

What an offensive argument, says the romantic. There are many systems of justice, and not all are suited to every people and culture. "Rights" will be given a different interpretation in different societies; the very idea of rights may not be suitable for all. Education must be different – suited to a people's particular character. And not everyone should be required to live in a liberal democracy. The form of government we call liberal democracy originated in the West and it's only the West that sees its system as inescapably the best. To try to impose it on others is patronizing and imperialistic. For different peoples, for different *races*, there must be different forms of rule.

Of course, those who entertain the romantic argument on community aren't all of one mind. Some are awash in romanticism. Others merely dabble. Charles Taylor dabbles. He cannot believe liberal democracy is *sufficient* for human flourishing and yet he continues to admire it. Thus, he supports the building of a Québécois way of life to distinguish the citizens of Quebec from other populations on the North American continent but hopes at the same time that the Quebec will *not* differ from other jurisdictions in its adherence to broad principles of liberal-democratic justice. In all his writings on Quebec, Taylor is looking for the halfway house.

LIBERALS FOR "CHOICE"

I said that the liberal likes to think of individuals freely choosing to identify with community. Liberals don't deny that one's skin colour, body type, or accent provoke certain reactions in others. Identification with community isn't always voluntary. Nevertheless, says the liberal, the good society should do all possible to enable an individual to escape harmful stereotyping. In the best regime, the individual will be able to choose whether to accept ascribed identifications. She will choose whether to work within her community of origin or to distance herself.

Liberals like Will Kymlicka argue that people will often choose to identify with a community because such identification is perceived as a good. Thus, according to Kymlicka, liberal society should foster conditions in which individuals can choose or reject their community with a good heart. (Or choose communities (in the plural); one might declare affiliation with more than one; people often do, as Kymlicka notes. In the "original position," one might ask for "an identity, or identities, specifics to be filled in later.")

Kymlicka's point is that the Canadian government should take reasonable care to protect minority ways of life. The argument has romantic overtones. But, from a strong romantic position, it's inadequate. Identification with a community is not merely one good thing among others. It is the condition of our humanity. It's the condition of our flourishing as individuals. It's not something we *choose*; it's what we *are*. Kymlicka's mistake is the classic liberal one: he supposes that there can be selves in abstraction from communities. It's Rawls's mistake. It's Locke's mistake. So the romantic argues.

TALKING CANADA

In 1972 Pierre Trudeau published a book of observations called *Conversation with Canadians*. "Conversation with Canadians." The phrase sounds ordinary enough. It suggests that Trudeau had formed some opinions about the country and wanted to get them out to a broader public. But in some scholarly circles the idea that one talks *about* a country is hopelessly old-fashioned.

The thing to say now is that Canada *is* the conversation. Trudeau, his interlocutors, and his readers were creating the country. Countries are conversations. Cultural minorities are conversations. This is Jeremy Webber's argument.

Webber approaches the idea by describing the difficulties Canadians had in drafting the "Canada clause" for the Charlottetown constitutional accord. The Canada clause was to have been something like a mission statement for the nation. Corporations have mission statements. Universities have them. Why shouldn't a country? It was to be a list of Canadian goals and values – the ones we all share – written in stirring language.

Excellent idea, you may say. Canada's constitutional documents are notably lacking in rhetoric. I've tried to persuade you that there's philosophical substance in the Constitution Act, 1867. But I'm certainly not going to argue that there's poetry in it. When it comes to constitutional rhetoric, the Americans are streets ahead of us. Strictly legalistic is Canada's style.

It proved extraordinarily difficult to draw up the clause. Adding the zing of rhetoric was the least of the problems. We couldn't agree on the substance. Webber's not surprised. In his opinion, a country's goals and values can't be captured by a list, or clause, no matter how inclusive. Rather the country's values unfold over time as people think – and talk – about what might be on such a list. The whole chorus of voices approving sections of the list, objecting to sections, objecting to the very existence of a list, described the Canada of that period. The chorus of different opinions was the nation. That's Webber's argument.

Of course, the chorus of Canadians talked then and talks today about many things, not just about politics and constitutions. We were talking before Confederation, we're talking today, and all the time we're creating the country. An interesting thesis! The question for us is this: What are the consequences for democracy?

Webber would say that, insofar as we see a nation or community as conversation, we're favouring democracy. All participate; all have the opportunity to influence the community's course of development. We constrict democracy, or stop it outright, when we rely on constitutional pronouncements, court orders, or decrees.

Jeremy Webber teaches in a faculty of law but, to judge from this book, has little faith in constitutions. He certainly says little about law. He doesn't recommend substantive constitutional reforms and says almost nothing about Parliament and parliamentary procedures. Shall we call Webber a romantic? Well, let's think. There's more to romanticism than distrust of political institutions. But certainly Webber has to be counted among the scholars who demean the formal institutions of liberal democracy.

Consider how our founders of the 1860s would respond to such a thesis. They'd have no problems with the idea of debate and dialogue. Call it conversation if you wish. They certainly wouldn't have difficulty with the notion that, in a democratic society, there are a great many different voices, opinions, and interests. They believed that diversity of opinion was the strength of a democracy.

But they'd surely ask searching questions about the procedures for conducting the conversation. They'd want to know whether there were mechanisms to preserve and honour dissenting voices. They'd wonder about security for the political minorities. About these matters Webber says little.

They'd worry especially about demagoguery. We all know that bullies can hog a conversation. Sometimes by force or bribery. Sometimes by charm and rhetoric. What protects the populace against the demagogue in Webber's populist program?

There's no doubt that it's satisfying to participate in a free-wheeling conversation. In Webber's conversations, each person will be busy realizing herself, expressing herself, communicating about everything and anything. It doesn't exactly matter. And all the time she'll be taking cues from others and reacting to expressions of approval or disapproval. She'll be asserting or acquiring an identity.

A conversation over the back fence is something one can walk away from. Webber clearly envisages the Canadian conversation as something more substantial, something that has political consequences. But he doesn't make it clear how political measures would be decided or ratified. How would you leave the kind of conversation Webber describes? (And would you have to abandon your identity if you left?) And supposing you didn't leave, how would you register your dissent? Short of shouting down your adversaries. Or shooting them.

Webber's given us a good description of free speech in democratic societies. He describes half of the democratic equation. What he's "talking" about is sometimes called the phenomenon of public opinion. Whatever we call it – conversation, public opinion – we shouldn't ignore its importance. I've suggested that the arena of public opinion may sometimes be bullying and inequalitarian. But I don't want to leave the impression that it isn't necessary. The stalwarts of the press and the political establishment sometimes dominate it, but it can also work to include people who have trouble making themselves heard in liberal democracy's formal institutions. Women were active in the public square before they had the vote. Visitors and transients participate. Non-voters. Extreme dissidents. Romantics!

But the liberal rejects the public square as the sufficient institution of our democracy. It's necessary, but not sufficient. Without the formal institutions of liberal democracy, public opinion – the conversation – is nothing more than the mob rule that men like George-Étienne Cartier feared: the herd trampling back and forth, ignoring minorities, bowing before the demagogue.

We need institutions where those making the formal decisions must answer to the public, where dissent is recorded, where citizens can complain about decisions and organize to reverse them and to oust from political office those who made them. We need parliaments that respect the rule of law and courts to enforce it. So the liberal contends. Given such institutions, *fruitful* conservation will flourish.

In Webber's scheme, there's no deliberation of the kind John A. Macdonald praised. No doubt the participants move from one topic to another. But it's the fact that they're talking, the fact of conversation, that's creating the community (and the participating selves). Not what's talked *about*. There's only talk. Canada has moved a long way from the great Age of Political Deliberation. Now, what are the consequences of that move? I wonder.

Canada as conversation, eh? Something to talk about!

13

The Romantic Artist in Her Lonely Garret

I said in previous chapters that we won't be able to think clearly about multiculturalism and citizenship until we shed the assumptions of right-centre-left. We won't understand the issues until we stop fighting the idea that Canada is a liberal democracy, much like the United States in broad outline, founded on principles of political equality.

So now that we're beyond right-centre-left, you're entitled to ask whether we've made much progress. What's the new picture on multiculturalism? A very good question! As the professor likes to say.

LIBERAL MULTICULTURALISM: REPRISE

The great issue for the liberal is this: How are humans to live together without exploiting and killing each other? The classic liberal answer is John Locke's. We must limit politics. We must take out of public life the contestations that occasion war. Especially we must prevent citizens from using ethnic affiliation, or family connection, or religion to claim exclusive privileges from the state or an exclusive right to the exercise of state power. Such claims are inherently objectionable as contrary to the principle of natural equality and are to be feared because they give rise to resentments that in the extreme set citizen against citizen in armed combat. People won't tolerate injustice. And in the modern world, injustice always seems to have at its core the perception that someone has been treated unequally.

Liberal democracies differ about means to limit the dangerous contention. Different histories and different patterns of settlement and immigration give rise to different remedies. But most refuse to allow church establishment. Most enforce a merit system in the competition for public offices. They strive for a representative political process. Religious preferences and particular affiliations are allowed in private life. As Jonathan Swift puts it in his sour fashion: "a man may be allowed to keep Poisons in his Closet, but not to vend them about as Cordials." In short, liberals distinguish between political life and private life. The legislative assembly and courts draw the boundary.

It's all so sensible, isn't it? (Asks the liberal.) And it's worked for so long. And it's given us – surely – a good life in this country. Civic nationalism takes pride in this good life. We're pleased with ourselves as a nation not because we're a superior gang, not because we're different, or "unique," or because we're working out the distinctive identity bequeathed us by history, but because we enjoy the Peace, Order, and Good Government to which all peoples aspire.

Is it sufficient? Does it satisfy our souls? Liberal democracies are pocketed with enclaves in private life, especially religious enclaves, which promise more for the soul. Those who live in them conduct themselves according to laws formulated before time began or laws that will find their fruition only at the end of days. They live, perhaps only one day a week, as if liberal democracy had never been invented. And such enclaves are permitted and protected. Is the formula sufficient? Probably not. Could we do better? It's doubtful. Do we have problems? Of course. Have we sometimes failed? Yes.

Should we be proud? Well, that's the question. The famous formulation runs as follows: liberal democracy is the worst regime except for all the others.

ROMANTIC NATIONALISM: REPRISE

The great question for the romantic is this: How can we ensure that all *flourish*? I've already said that, insofar as the romantics espouse democracy, they're reluctant to lay down constricting principles and formulas. As Judith Shklar says at one point about the communitarian romantics: "To submit to politics was an act of resigning to actuality and as such an abandonment of romanticism." But romantics can dream – none better. Here is the political dream of one romantic, the poet and philosopher Schiller, as described by Isaiah Berlin: "How are men to be reconciled to each other? ... Schiller goes back, not very effectively or convincingly, to the Kantian principle that if we are rational, if we are like the Greeks, if we are harmonious, if we understand ourselves, if we understand what freedom is, if we understand what morality is, if we understand what the pleasures and the heavenly delight of artistic creation is, then surely we shall somehow achieve a harmonious relation with other creators, other artists equally concerned not with mowing other men down, not with crushing them, but with living with them in some happy, united creative world."

As the song says: "What the world needs now is love, sweet love." Along with, if we believe Schiller, a strong dash of modern German art. In the best world we will not only be free individuals but will all get along together in one pacific community. That's equality. That's democracy. Berlin doesn't find this utopianism convincing, apparently. But we're entitled to ask: Are such dreams a serious challenge to liberalism?

The answer is no, and yes.

WHATEVER HAPPENED TO THE ROMANTIC IN HER LONELY GARRET?

Now we face a difficulty. By reputation, romantics are not only apolitical; they're anti-social. They're notorious for their anti-social behaviour! They delight in offending the public, the masses, the crowds of "philistines" who profess to enjoy romantic art but (says the romantic) in fact understand nothing and support art merely for the frisson of occasional association with bohemia. Romantics hanker for the lonely garret, the wilderness, distant countries (distant eras!), the simple life far from the madding crowd. They desire to be alone ("I vant to be alone," as Garbo says), superior to all and gratifyingly despised and rejected. Alone: all on his or her oddyknocky. This is a very common picture of the romantic!

But recall the argument in the preceding chapters. We have been entertaining the idea that the romantic is some kind of communitarian, a believer in affiliation and identification with one's peers. Have we gone off the rails somewhere? Perhaps we can take refuge in the idea that the romantic movement is a bundle of contradictions. We'll say that it promiscuously embraces the extremes of individualism *and* the extremes of cultural immersion. Or perhaps we can find evidence to suggest that the movement begins by espousing individualism and only later recommends community. To explore this last hypothesis would require thorough study of the history of ideas. Shklar provides some support for it.

I think that there's considerable truth to the idea that romanticism embraces contradictions. The movement was born in the democratic revolt against the *ancien régime* in France. (Or perhaps it occasioned that turmoil.) It continues today in highly political demonstrations against the governments of the Western nations, and against global institutions, and in these actions romantics describe themselves as democrats, friends of "the people," friends of "the masses." In short, a versatile romantic can work up a storm of argument about the necessity of being true to the self while also waxing emotional about making common cause to befriend the downtrodden. Just as it suits her. And whether she goes home to her lonely garret or rushes to the barricades, she opposes the "powers that be," the established institutions and elites. She rejects liberalism.

But though the "bundle of contradictions" hypothesis is promising, let me follow another line of thought. The last chapter made the strong claim that romantics do not see a contradiction between individualism and communal affiliation. Liberals see a contradiction; romantics don't. (It all seems so clear to the liberal. Either you're standing alone against the mob. Or you're running with the crowd. You can't do both at once!) Typical liberal blindness! says the romantic. The liberal fails to see that individuality develops *only* in the context of community. In the good regime, all realize individual identity through adherence to communal norms. They know themselves insofar as they see their actions and attitudes reflected in the actions and attitudes of others.

This is the challenging idea in romanticism today. This is a major cause of romantic dissatisfaction with liberal democracy.

(Note that we're now in a position to answer the question posed at the beginning of this chapter: "What's the new picture?" Once we shed right-centre-left, we're free to see on the horizon a more thoroughgoing challenge to liberal democracy.) We must consider one more development.

To say that the self is realized only in and through communal interactions is just a step away from saying that there is no self. There is only community. There are indeed only the interactions. In the last pages of *The Roots of Romanticism*, Berlin says: the "essence of the romantic movement, so far as I can see [is] will and man as an activity, as something which cannot be described because it is perpetually creating; you must not even say that it is creating itself, for there is no self, there is only movement. That is the heart of romanticism."

"There is no self." Hmm. We have already encountered something like this notion. According to Jeremy Webber, Canadians' conversation about Canadian values does not result in a "list" of values. Canada's "mission statement" is always being torn up, patched, rewritten, discarded, and retrieved and it's the process of tearing up and rewriting that is important. A difficult thought! We may talk about Canada's "foundations," but we don't pour the concrete, so to speak. Now we're being asked to consider whether in a "conversation" there are conversers. There's talk, certainly, but are there talkers? There are no selves, says Berlin. There are interactions but no "actors."

Here's Berlin describing the philosopher Fichte on the self (Fichte, in turn, is extrapolating from David Hume): "... when he looked within himself as people normally do, when he introspected, he discovered a great many sensations, emotions, fragments of memory, of hope and fear – all kinds of small psychological units – but he failed to perceive any entity which could justly be called a self, and therefore concluded that the self was not a thing, not an object of direct perception, but perhaps simply a name for the concatenation of experiences out of which human personality and human history were formed, simply a kind of string which held together the onions, except that there was no string."

"Except that there was no string." Very amusing. There is no self. Ha, ha. It's difficult for the liberal to think of absence of "self," especially absence of self that is associated with will and creativity. But let me suggest that the notion is more familiar than one might suppose at first blush. Part of our problem is that I've introduced it by referring, if only indirectly, to philosophers like Fichte and Hume. I did it because my mentor, Berlin, introduces the idea in this way and because such an introduction traces the notion to the romantic movement. But what if instead of chattering about stringless onions, and "no self," I had boldly said that the theory of social determinism demeans the idea of the self as conceived by the Enlightenment? Now we're on familiar ground. Every social scientist is acquainted with arguments to suggest that individuals are the product of their social and economic environment. It's said, for example, that youngsters who offend against the law have been let down by society, or by their parents. They came from inner-city schools; they were abused. As the kids say in Leonard Bernstein's *West Side Story*, "we're depraved on accounta we're deprived." (Imagine joyous music: "We're depraved, we're depraved! La di, da, da, da! We're depraved on accounta we're deprived.")

If we believe Berlin, the romantic movement gives rise to the doctrine of social determinism. It wasn't all a matter of sulking in garrets, defending revolutionary barricades, and bemoaning lost continents, lost countries, and lost loves. In the course of those activities, romantic thinkers developed dark and challenging ideas about the human experience. Ideas that had been ignored by the liberal Enlightenment. Ideas of great power, which are taken up and popularized by modern sociology, psychology, and historiography. The romantic movement culminates in the teaching that the independent, decision-making individual of the liberal Enlightenment is a fiction.

Of course, the idea that deprivation breeds depravity isn't usually taken to mean that there's no self at all. The liberal's ready to compromise on this issue. Environment plays a role. Who can deny it? But the determining, deciding self is surely present. Liberals are always so reasonable and so ready to compromise! They underestimate the romantic argument. At its strongest the romantic argument says there's only activity, only the concatenation of experiences.

EVIL FUTURES AGAIN

Liberal democracy was designed for adults – independent, intelligent, and responsible. It's for women and men in charge of their faculties, able to make decisions prudently with an eye to consequences for themselves and for others, and prepared to act in accordance with their decisions.

From the seventeenth century there were arguments to suggest that many people – some men and most women – are not capable of the prudent intelligence required by liberal democracy. Thus, there were arguments for restricting the franchise and limiting eligibility for jury duty and public office as well as access to higher education. And so on. But gradually the logic of popular sovereignty, the rule of law, and the natural-right assumptions of Locke and Hobbes worked their way into our hearts and minds. It was never supposed that all were equally intelligent, and equally prudent, of course. Indeed, it was never supposed that every last citizen had even the minimal intelligence and prudence. Some people cannot look after themselves, let alone others. The suggestion was that most met the requirements. Most people can understand a judge's disquisition on the difference between first-degree murder and second-degree murder. Most people can understand what's within the realm of the possible in politics and what's just pie in the sky. Most people can rise above the limits of their background to grasp the idea of the common good. People in general are shrewd enough, prudent enough. And, given good institutions, they can maintain the vigilance that is the price of liberty. And so liberal democracies extended the franchise, opened opportunities for women, lifted restrictions on higher education, and introduced the merit principle into competitions for the public service.

Now the argument is that gender, origin, religion, and tribe are the whole story. According to the romantic, there's no shrewd, prudent self, standing outside. There is only the concatenation of experiences. There's only will and activity. If the argument's right, liberal democracy is not possible. It never was. Its apparent success was freakish. Now the lie is exposed and we're entering the real world. The days of liberal democracy are numbered.

Every day sees new evidence of erosion. But can this dark message be something Berlin himself accepts? Isaiah Berlin, the famous defender of liberalism?

In the final pages of *The Roots of Romanticism*, Berlin pulls back from the idea that there are no selves. He doesn't, in this book, give a reason for pulling back. But let's retreat with him. It's cowardly to say that one can't cope with the "no-self" argument. But let's be cowards. And honestly, everyone – if there is an every "one" – experiences the soupy concatenation, but usually "one" worries about it only first thing in the morning, and then gets on with the day.

SAYING GOODBYE TO BERLIN

Berlin pulls back, but he doesn't let the argument go altogether. He suggests that to open the mind, if only a little, to the idea that there are no selves is probably good for liberals. It takes them down a peg. It keeps them from being too *self*-satisfied. It shakes their confidence in the power of reason. And that's salutary. Or so he suggests. We owe to romanticism, he says, "the notion that there are many values, and that they are incompatible; the whole notion of pluralism, of inexhaustibility, of the imperfection of all human answers and arrangements." He argues, in brief, that romanticism makes liberalism more tolerant: "... a rather peculiar situation has arisen. Here are the romantics, whose chief burden is to destroy ordinary tolerant life, to destroy philistinism, to destroy common sense, to destroy the peaceful avocations of men, to raise everybody to some passionate level of self-expressive experience, of such a kind as perhaps only divinities, in older works of literature, were supposed to manifest ... and yet, as a result of making clear the existence of a plurality of values, as a result of driving wedges into the notion of ... the single answer to all questions ... we arrive at an appreciation of the necessity of tolerating others ..." There it is: romanticism teaches tolerance. That's Berlin's argument in these crucial last pages. He's suggesting that liberalism can live with romanticism and even benefit from it. But let's consider.

What Berlin fears above all is what he and others call "monism." "Monism" is supremely intolerant. A monist philosophy imposes a "single answer to all questions"; a monist *regime* ruthlessly destroys all who refuse to comply with the one answer. *The Roots of Romanticism* provides two separate and incompatible accounts of the origins of monism. I noted above that Berlin sometimes speaks of fascism – monism par excellence – as an "inheritor of romanticism." There are passages in which he suggests that the romantic movement's hostility to constitutionalism and its mockery of all things liberal, its scorn for political compromise and disdain for ordinary human aspirations, destroyed the political bulwarks against human cruelty in Europe and prepared the way for the most devastating forms of monism history has known, the twentieth-century totalitarianisms. I find this argument convincing.

But there are other passages in which he seems to say that *liberalism* is monist and the progenitor of the monist tyrannies. When he argues, for example, that romanticism helpfully drives wedges into liberal confidence in "the single answer to all questions," he is treating liberalism as a monist philosophy. This was James Tully's contention, you may remember; liberalism is monist; classical liberalism is cruelly intolerant because it demands conformity to one great principle.

If we follow this line of thought, we are led to conclude that it is not the Counter-Enlightenment that gave us fascism and communism, but the Enlightenment. Not romanticism, but liberalism. What the world needs to prevent the killing fields, the gulags, the ethnic cleansings, the jihads, is more romanticism!

Perhaps it's time to part company with Berlin. I don't believe that liberalism is intolerant. It had its origins in the attempt to accommodate pluralism while constraining pluralism's sometimes devastating effects on public life. Liberalism was, and remains, a supremely tolerant political prescription.

In the preceding chapters, I described Aristotle's three regimes as "simple" monarchy, "simple" aristocracy, and "simple" democracy. The simple regimes are, to change the terminology, monist regimes. And Aristotle and most certainly his modern disciples understand that because they are monist they are prone to tyranny. The remedy, I said, the *liberal* remedy, is the mixed regime, the mixture of monarchy, aristocracy, and democracy. It takes one form in the ancient world and another in the modern, but whatever the form it is meant to prevent dangerous monism. Liberalism and liberal democracy prescribe a mixed regime in order to save us from monist tyranny.

The United States today is a mixed regime. Canada is a mixed regime. These countries enjoy Enlightenment constitutions. And though they're far from perfect, they support pluralism and haven't yet delivered us to the cruel tyrannies that Europe had to endure in the last century.

14

The Three Deaths of the Canadian Constitution

At some point, perhaps as early as the 1960s, academic historians stopped writing about the Canadian constitution and national events and turned to "history from below," the study of localities, regions, ethnic groups, women's lives, labour, and so on. Jack Granatstein describes the new approach in *Who Killed Canadian History?* It's not part of Granatstein's argument that historians should ignore history from below. He admits that in the old days the academics had shamefully neglected localities and groups. But he does regret the loss of Canadian national history.

With national history gone there passed from the scene an important vehicle for the transmission of information about parliamentary institutions and principles. This was the first death. A generation of Canadian scholars grew up without knowledge of the Glorious Revolution, popular sovereignty, the principles for which Americans fought the Revolution, the idea of liberal democracy. They didn't know and they didn't care. There was no fresh examination of these things. No one said, "Let me see for myself. I want to read those constitutional documents; I'm not content with secondary sources." Study of the constitution wasn't the cutting edge.

The philosophers brought on the second death. And here's the paradox. They killed the constitution by writing about it. Their larger-than-life picture of national history provoked radical dissatisfaction with our present institutions.

And then, still in the 1960s, in the "summer of love," while Canadian youngsters were dancing in the parks and singing songs of liberation, while the historians were packing away their books on law and constitutions, while the philosophers were summoning the great minds of the ancient and modern worlds to demonstrate the deficiencies of liberal democracy, the politicians sat down to make a few adjustments to the British North America Act. And as they worked, they found more and more to change, and more and more reasons for dissatisfaction. Thus began the third death.

THE MORNING AFTER

Three strikes and you're out. But three deaths and you're dead? Perhaps not.

Consider the fate of the Charlottetown constitutional accord. Drafted in 1991–92, it looked to many like the sovereign remedy for Canada's ills. It had something for everyone. Supposedly. It reformed the parliamentary system, the Supreme Court, the Charter of Rights and Freedoms, the amending formula, and the division of legislative powers. It gave aboriginals self-government. It defined (or redefined) the Canadian nationality.

Almost everyone in the political mainstream supported it: the federal and provincial governments, the major opposition parties at the federal level, the governments of the Territories, and the major aboriginal organizations. And yet in the national referendum of 1992 the majority of Canadians said "no" to this cure-all package. Why? I'm not sure we understand to this day. In a referendum it's always easier to say "no." And Charlottetown was vulnerable just because it offered so much. It was a package deal; take it all or leave it. The majority made the safe choice: "leave it."

We can't conclude that by voting down Charlottetown Canadians were expressing satisfaction with the constitutional status quo. Both sides were arguing for thoroughgoing reform. The No side (which included the Reform party, the Bloc Québécois, the National Action Committee on the Status of Women, and other prominent groups) said that the reforms proposed by the Yes side were not the right ones, or that the package as a whole did not go far enough. The fact is that everyone who was anyone – the No side as much as the Yes – was arguing that the parliamentary process, security for rights, our present democracy were unsatisfactory. The old constitution no longer worked. We needed a new one. A New Canada.

And then we didn't get a new one. And we aren't likely to. Most observers are of the opinion that the era of "mega-constitutional reform" is over. There will probably never be another proposal for constitutional reform on the scale of Charlottetown. Indeed, it now appears that under the 1982 constitutional amending formula it is difficult to secure even minor constitutional amendments insofar as they affect national institutions. The long campaign for a new constitution may be over.

The question for us in this chapter is whether the campaign has damaged Canadians' confidence in democracy. I think it has. We've been wounded.

Think about it. We were riding the romantic rails. In the run-up to the referendum it seemed that every good political reform was there for the asking. Strong democracy, aboriginal self-government, an end to poverty, better health care, recognition of this, affirmation of that. If we could just figure out how to fit it all into one constitutional document.

And then the dreams and passions, the romance, collapsed. It was quite a let-down. A "morning after." Canadians were "left behind" with the old institutions of 1867 and 1982.

How have we done since? We're muddling through. We're not happy, but we're carrying on. I now begin to think that we'll do better if we understand that arguments for a new constitution come at a high price. Too much of the talk on constitutional reform still centres on the idea of starting up the bus again. Too much is given to the notion that our salvation might still lie in mega-constitutional reform. We need to think about what happened to us during the years of the constitutional odyssey.

Let me say it again. Though disdain for politics is a perennial theme in romanticism, romantics can't leave politics alone. As Shklar says, "the sporadic desire to find self-expression in political activity still animates romantic souls." The "Byronic impulse" is not dead. In this passage ("still animates") Shklar is writing about the 1950s. But the observation is true of our time. At moments of revolution and at moments of political founding, the romantic feels the call. And at those moments his actions do not seem to him a mere matter of Byronic "self-expression." He becomes the champion of the people, building a new political order.

"Who gets what, when, and how" can be left to the philistines. But to create a new order – that's a task for the artist, for the ardent, the young at heart, the visionaries. Or so the romantic contends. I suggested in previous chapters that romantics enjoy destroying old regimes more than building new ones. Even so, when the door into the garden opens, when the breeze from a better world blows – the romantic calls up a new file and begins to draft a constitution.

It may sound far-fetched to compare the program of constitutional reform in the Charlottetown accord to the French Declaration of the Rights of Man and Citizen and similar revolutionary documents. But, yes, I think that in a small way, in a modest Canadian way, the breeze from a better world was blowing in 1992. The Charlottetown Accord promised a new founding. And everyone capable of romance responded.

Prudence went by the boards. And scruples. And sober second thought. And all the dour liberal virtues.

"RECOGNITION" AND "PROCESS": BUZZ, BUZZ

Consider Charlottetown's "Canada clause" – the section that gave Jeremy Webber so much trouble, the one that is supposed to define the Canadian identity by "recognizing" the signal elements of Canadian political life. After 1982, Canadians milled around the communal hive trying to repair the damage done by Trudeau's callous treatment of Quebec. The remedy that suggested itself was to insert in the constitution a clause recognizing Quebec's distinctiveness. In the Charlottetown Draft Legal Text of October 1992, the "distinct society" clause appears as a subsection in the Canada clause, one of eight subsections. Why eight? Well, other groups wanted to get in on the deal. Why only eight? I'm sure that there would have been more if the debate had gone on longer. Aboriginals, official-language minorities, ethic and religious minorities, feminists, and proponents of regionalism are recognized in the Canada clause on the same footing as Quebec. The fact is that the original project – recognition of Quebec in order to heal the breach between Canada and Quebec – got lost somewhere along the way.

The groups that jostled Quebec for a place on the list weren't fighting over empty honours. The mention of a group or a group's objectives (or mention of an "identity" or a nationality) in a constitutional document can be used in the courts and in the arena of public opinion to argue for publicly funded privileges and benefits. To give one example: a clause affirming equality of the sexes can be used by feminist groups to persuade the courts to countenance affirmative-action programs for women. A clause affirming the equality of "every individual" can be used to argue in the legislature and in the courts for same-sex spousal benefits.

Constitutional law is traditionally considered "superior law," meaning, for one thing, that it defines the standard of fairness that guides legislatures and courts. Of course, a constitutional text can be interpreted in different ways. Mention in the constitution doesn't guarantee a group's success. A court might find that the equality of all individuals does *not* legitimate same-sex benefits. But as groups in Canada now understand, it's game over if you have no constitutional clause. Get the text today, get the clause, and tomorrow work for your preferred interpretation. For most groups, that's the program.

Feminists in English-speaking Canada argued that Quebec's "distinct society" clause might be used to demean the position of women in Quebec and perhaps elsewhere in the rest of Canada. They demanded their own Canada-clause mention, which reads: "Canadians are committed to the equality of male and female persons." Feminists in Quebec argued stoutly that no court in their province would ever interpret the phrase "distinct society" in a fashion to curtail women's equality. They said that feminism was streets ahead in Quebec and that indeed feminism was part of the very distinctiveness of Quebec's distinct society. Of course, the anglophone feminists knew that Quebec's record on feminism was strong. They made their argument in order to get "their clause" (already entrenched in the Canadian Charter of Rights and Freedoms in almost the same words) affirmed again in the new document. Making assurance doubly sure.

Thus the quarrels went. Jostle, jostle. Haggle, haggle. To repeat: listing in the Canada clause, or mention of one's traditions and projects in *any* section of the constitution, is not an empty honour, a mere matter of status. There are concrete benefits at stake. Now let's think for a minute.

The romantic nationalists tell us that groups should recognize each other in a mutual, "multilogic" fashion. "A" should recognize "B." "B" should recognize "A." Thus both are affirmed and both flourish. Indeed, the theorists suggest that *all* should be recognized. All should have prizes, as Alice says. But when many or all are recognized, does recognition have the same cachet? Because constitutional recognition is valuable many want it. But when many have it, what's it worth? As Gilbert and Sullivan put it in *The Gondoliers*: "When everybody's somebody, then no one's anybody."

That's one problem. A more serious one is that, as the value of "recognition" goes down, the value of constitutions and constitutionalism is called in question. Let me put this idea in the form of a general observation. When a constitution describes and recognizes the objectives of particular groups, the distinction between statute law and the constitution breaks down. (Some romantics: "Hooray!") There's no reason to suppose the constitution "superior" law. Constitutional law, shmonstitutional law: it's all made by special interests, eh? It's all a matter of "who gets what, when, how." What's "superior"? What's to respect?

I suggested above that in settled democracies the constitution embodies (or ought to embody) the citizens' idea of justice or fairness. To say this is not to say that the constitution is the citizens' only source for ideas of fairness. Not at all. And it's not to say that everyone is equally enthusiastic about everything in the constitution. The argument is merely that in most liberal democracies the constitution is accepted as the rulebook for managing the regime. Thus, though democracies modify their constitutions from time to time, they usually make only incremental changes. And those incremental changes are made only after almost everyone is satisfied that the reform meets with public approval. That is, only when it is reasonably clear that the public's ideas about what's fair have changed. Recall the doctrine of popular sovereignty.

In the case of Charlottetown, the participating groups obviously did not agree about what's fair. They were making competing demands, and they made those demands in the hope of *changing* the public's mind. They weren't following a change in popular opinion. They were trying to force change.

Here's the irony. Throughout the Charlottetown debates, activists argued that what was required was a process of constitutional reform that respected popular sovereignty. They said that the new constitution had to be submitted to the people for their approval. Politicians had to defer to the sovereign people. And yet the activists were trying to change the sovereign, trying to manipulate it. For particular, partisan effect, to benefit some groups at the expense of others, to ensure that certain partial and political programs were favoured.

Even a seemingly innocuous reform will reduce confidence in constitutionalism if it appears to be associated with a particular agenda. It might be argued that the clause affirming the equality of male and female persons expresses the thinking of all right-minded persons, liberal and romantic. (Of course.) So what objection can there be to putting it in the constitution? And yet there were objections. The use that had been made of the similar clause in the Charter suggested that it might be cited to support programs of affirmative action, about which – in Rainer Knopff's phrase – reasonable people may reasonably disagree. French Canadians and some others were offended by the idea that the clause was required to protect women from the machinations of nationalists.

In short, even a clause that seems to apply to all citizens even-handedly may carry a stinger. I believe that the haggling and wrangling that accompanied the making of the Charlottetown Accord impressed this notion firmly on the public mind. And so the idea that there's a distinction between constitutional law and statute law began to slip away. And with it the idea of constitutionalism. And confidence in liberal democracy.

One difference between the two kinds of law would remain. When the Charlottetown Accord was formally entrenched as an amendment to the Constitution Act 1867, it would be harder to change than ordinary statute law. Thus, inequities would be cast in constitutional stone. Unfairness heaped on unfairness!

Of course, it's an old argument of the anti-institutional romantics that there is no distinction between constitutions and statutes. We've already met it. Everything's politics and politics is a low business. Constitutionalism and liberal democracy profess to be systems that acknowledge the equality of all citizens; in fact, they legitimate rule by particular elites, the fat cats, the philistines, the capitalists, the bourgeoisie. That's the contention. The very fact of constitutions imperils equality, freedom, and democracy. And if I haven't admitted it before, I will now. There's some truth to the charge. Liberals know this as much as romantics. Or they should. Even the minimal constitution bolsters a certain way of life and protects a certain kind of citizen.

Romantics can't hang on to this insight. They lost it during the heady days of the French Revolution. They lost it at terrible moments in the twentieth century. And they lost it in the Charlottetown debates. Let's turn to the liberal side.

Liberals argue that there must be constitutions. There must be foundations. There must be a rulebook. It's the *lack* of these things that truly imperils freedom, equality, and democracy. Without a rulebook the bullies take over. Then we're on the slippery slope to civil war and tyranny. In the worst case, tanks and rockets replace arguments and deliberation. We've seen *this* argument before. The point to note is that prudent liberals agree with the anti-institutional romantics to a limited extent. A constitution is likely to support to a certain way of life. But the romantic concludes from this insight that constitutions should be abolished – or written to romantic specifications. The liberal concludes that constitutions should embody few principles. And should be changed seldom.

Especially, insofar as possible, says the liberal, constitutions should refrain from "recognizing" the political objectives of particular groups. Attempts to define national character should be avoided. Rhetoric should be avoided. Just the bare description of institutions and principles, please. And go easy on the principles.

The good constitution will lay down the formula for a parliamentary or congressional system. If it's a federal regime, there'll be a section on the division of legislative powers and an amending formula. A bill of rights is optional. There might be a preamble mentioning the rule of law. Of course, historical and political considerations will always come into play in the process of drafting. The liberal is pragmatic, ready to compromise even in the matter of constitution making. But the general rule is this: the bare-bones constitution is best because it's the least likely to legitimate relations of domination and subordination.

POPULAR SOVEREIGNTY: JUST ONCE MORE

In 1992 the haggling groups, parties, and governments agreed to drop the whole mess in the public's lap. The Charlottetown

Accord would be referred to the people in a national referendum. We're back with our old dilemma! How to consult the people about a new (or thoroughly renovated) constitution? It should be done. But how?

In the heat of the Charlottetown debates, it was said repeatedly that the people had been ignored in the making of the Constitution Act, 1982 and ignored again in the making of the Meech Lake constitutional accord (drafted 1987; deceased 1990). Peter Russell was one scholar who made this contention. I said in earlier chapters that the Fathers of Confederation did *not* ignore the issue of popular consultation. And I would make a similar claim about 1982, 1990, and 1992. Popular consultation was on everyone's mind. It's true that there were no national referendums in 1982 and 1990. But yes, political interest groups, constitutional lawyers, academics, governments, parties, committees, and ad hoc groups of citizens were on the scene, buzzing with proposals, brandishing drafts, urging particular clauses. All of them publicized their appeals. There was discussion of constitutional issues large and small in the news for decades *before* 1982. And after, to the very day of the 1992 referendum. And anyone who wanted to join in the debates, or just sound off, or announce to all the country, "I'll be revenged on the whole pack of you," was very welcome. The political elites encouraged all this attention to the constitutional process; they courted it; they arranged forums, and committees, and schedules of consultation. Constitution making was a national preoccupation. Not to everyone's taste. But for many, an excellent, excellent adventure.

So the people were consulted. But were they happy about the fact of consultation? No! For one thing, as I've said, individuals and groups were seized by the anxious fear that a political program antithetical to their interests would be entrenched. Feminists would rule. Or wouldn't rule. The aboriginals would run the country. Or would be ignored yet again. The French would refuse to acknowledge provincial equality. The English would once more assert their insufferable sense of superiority. Nasty sentiments began to emerge during these debates, which Canadians – who are truly a moderate and tolerant people – strove manfully and womanfully to suppress.

Let's look at one more aspect of these famous, or infamous, debates. This is my last topic. The debates were cast as a contest between "the people" and "the elites." Or between "the people and the "politicians." And a curious idea took root. It was said that *only* the people should draft and ratify constitutions. The politicians should retire from the scene. The people should run the whole show. It's an engaging idea. And as I don't need to say, highly romantic.

Activists argued that the process of making a new constitution was "too important to leave to the regular partisan-dominated political process." Get politicians and parties out of the business. Leave constitution making to "the people," the "ordinary people" of Canada.

Thus, it's not surprising that during the Charlottetown debates almost no one argued that *Parliament* and the provincial legislatures represent the people for the purpose of ratification. You'll remember that at the time of Confederation the majority of legislators said that, "Parliament is the people." The contention was that Parliament is the voice of all inhabitants of the country, all affected by law, and that the majority formed by parliamentary debate is more inclusive than the raw majority of a referendum. Parliament is an arena designed to honour dissent; parliamentary deliberation thus has more legitimacy. We do not need to consider here whether this argument about Parliament offers sufficient reason to prefer ratification by legislative fiat. The important point now is that this argument was absent in the Charlottetown debates.

The accord was too important to leave to Parliament and the politicians. That was the argument. But some went further. They suggested that even the nation's day-to-day business is too important to leave to politicians. Canadians should banish parties and politicians altogether. Even the making of statute law should be done by "the people." In the run-up to the 1992 referendum, arguments for consensus and for direct democracy received a decided boost. As one theorist put it: "the parliamentary process is adversarial and majoritarian, the antithesis of a process that not only hears all voices but takes all experiences and aspirations into account." Activists who took this line usually said little about the processes that would replace elections and parliamentary deliberation. But we have seen that romantics have their reasons for silence. Forms of participation should always be in play; they emerge in the course of policy debates.

Think about it this way. By 1990, in Eastern Europe and the former Soviet Union, the idea of living in a "people's democracy" where the government speaks for all had become anathema to the inhabitants. How ironic that, in the very years in which the people of those countries were struggling to establish competitive party systems and representative legislatures and responsible governments, Canadians were flirting with arguments for the abolition of political parties and the demotion of legislatures.

THREE FUNERALS AND A WEDDING

Well, we've had the funerals. Where's the wedding? If you know, friends, get me an invitation.

Sources

CHAPTER ONE

When did we put on the "overcoat"? Sometime in the 1960s, I'd say. It wasn't worn and bunchy then. It was new, smart – the latest fashion.

Here's part of the story. Before the 1960s, Canadians defined themselves in terms of their political institutions: Canada was a federal nation with a parliamentary form of government. And most people considered that something to be modestly proud of. Then we changed our minds. Or some of us did – and they taught others. There were books and articles. University courses. The new ideas caught on. Political leaders began to pay attention. There were more books and articles. Not all Canadians adopted the new perspective. But almost everyone came to know about it.

We now defined ourselves in terms of "culture" – habits of mind and heart – rather than institutions. And we began to lose confidence in institutions, and in parliamentary liberal democracy. I believe that the change started with one book – Seymour Martin Lipset's *The First New Nation*, published in New York in 1963.

Lipset compared Americans and Canadians using categories ("pattern-variables") made famous by the sociologist Talcott Parsons. He concluded that Canadians are less "achievement-oriented," less "universalistic," less egalitarian, and less "self-oriented." Or to put the same thing in positive terms, Canadians are more inclined than Americans to treat people in terms of inherited characteristics. We put personal attributes and relationships ahead of merit. We look at particular circumstances (we're less likely to apply standards across the board). We're more deferential (less egalitarian), and – not least important – we are more likely to put the collectivity, that is, the community, ahead of individual interests.

Lipset pointed out that the differences were small. He insisted that there was a strong cultural similarity between English-speaking Canada and the United States. But for the professors of comparative political culture, those small differences loomed large. Achievement, universality, equality, individualism: these are terms associated the political culture of liberalism. Lipset had told us who we were! In a word, we were *less liberal* than Americans (liberal in the classic, Lockean sense).

See also Lipset's "Revolution and Counterrevolution: Canada and the United States," in Thomas Ford, ed., *The Revolutionary Theme in Contemporary America* (Lexington: University of kentucky Press 1965). Over the years Lipset pursued and elaborated the thesis in a number of publications. See, for example, *Continental Divide* (New York: Routledge 1990).

Lipset's picture was strongly supported by Gad Horowitz in an influential article that appeared at about the same time. In "Conservatism, Liberalism, and Socialism in Canada: an Interpretation," *Canadian Journal of Economics and Political Science* 32:2 (1966), Horowitz, too, argued that Canadians were more deferential and more oriented to the collectivity. He did not use the "pattern-variables" but relied on the powerful model of the march of political ideologies (right-centre-left) derived from Louis Hartz (and ultimately from Marx). Lipset's pattern-variables promised only to describe; right-centre-left purported to explain and predict. If Lipset had told us who we were, Horowitz told us why we could not have been otherwise. And what we might become.

For Louis Hartz, see *The Liberal Tradition in America* (New York: Harcourt, Brace and World 1955), and Hartz et al., *The Founding of New Societies: Studies in the History of the United States, Latin America, South Africa, Canada, and Australia* (New York: Harcourt, Brace and World 1964).

With the publication of Horowitz's "Liberalism, Conservatism, and Socialism," an industry was born. According to H.D. Forbes, "any overview of Canadian political thought or political culture must reckon with Horowitz's adaption of Hartz, for it is one of the few things in the field that everyone has read and remembers." Forbes, "Hartz-Horowitz at Twenty: Nationalism, Toryism and Socialism in Canada and the United States," *Canadian Journal of Political Science* 20:2 (1987). The commentary on Hartz-Horowitz is extensive – books, articles, theses, responses, rejoinders, and amendments. Forbes's notes are helpful. I'll mention only two standard textbooks, familiar to all students of political science: David Bell and Lorne Tepperman, *The Roots of Disunity: A Look at Canadian Political Culture* (Toronto: McClelland and Stewart 1979); and William Christian and Colin Campbell, *Political Parties and Ideologies in Canada*, 4th ed. (Toronto: McGraw-Hill Ryerson 1996). Horowitz himself wrote further articles and book essays; his original article has been reprinted several times in full and in abbreviated form.

George Grant's *Lament for a Nation* (1965) amplified the picture again. Grant relied on an analysis of culture (literature, ideas, beliefs) rather than institutions and has undoubtedly contributed to our lack of confidence in liberal democracy. Indeed, Grant tells us why we *should* not be liberal, that is, why we should not value merit, universal standards, equality, and individual rights. Grant's commentators, disciples, and disseminators outnumber Horowitz's. (Horowitz is among them.) The influence of Grant and Horowitz is explored further in chapters below.

Right-left-centre is still in vogue. See David V.J. Bell, "Political Culture in Canada," in Michael Whittington and Glen Williams, ed., *Canadian Politics in the 21st Century* (Scarborough, Ont.: Nelson 2000); and David Taras's Introduction to Taras and Beverly Rasporich, ed., *A Passion for Identity: An Introduction to Canadian Studies*, 3rd ed. (Scarborough, Ont.: Nelson 1997). The first generation of the new millennium is being fitted out with the old overcoat!

In *Canada's Origins: Liberal, Tory, or Republican?* (Ottawa: Carleton University Press 1995) Peter Smith and I republished Gad Horowitz's "Conservatism, Liberalism, and Socialism," along with essays calling Horowitz's thesis in question. Two chapters in Mark Charlton and Paul Barker, ed., *Crosscurrents: Contemporary Issues*, 3rd ed. (Scarborough, Ont.: Nelson 1998) go at the issue yet again. Nelson Wiseman takes up the cudgels for

Horowitz in "Tory-touch Liberalism: Political Culture in Canada." Peter Smith and I respond in "The 'Tory Touch' Thesis: Bad History, Poor Political Science."

That the Horowitz thesis retains its hold is suggested by its use in Paul M. Sniderman, Joseph F. Fletcher, Peter H. Russell, and Philip E. Tetlock, *The Clash of Rights, Liberty, Equality and Legitimacy in Pluralist Democracy* (New Haven, Conn.: Yale University Press 1996), where it is accepted as the authoritative account of Canada's origins despite the fact that the study's survey data do not bear it out.

Indeed, surveys provide little support for Lipset or Horowitz. The patterns of behaviour described by Lipset and the ideological attitudes described by Horowitz do not show up. The *Clash of Rights* survey, one of the most extensive comparisons of Canadian and American political culture, finds only negligible differences. Another important comparison of Canada and the United States, Neil Nevitte and Roger Gibbins, *New Elites in Old States: Ideologies in the Anglo-American Democracies* (Toronto: Oxford University Press 1990), comes to a similar conclusion: Canadian and American cultures are strikingly similar. (The Nevitte-Gibbins study includes Britain, Australia, and New Zealand, as well as Canada and the United States.) Paul Sniderman notes on the back cover of *New Elites*: "This book makes a major claim – that the Anglo-American democracies ... share a fundamentally similar political culture." Both *Clash of Rights* and *New Elites* are addressed to the general reader. Tables, graphs, and statistical tests are present in abundance, enough to satisfy the mavins, but the plain English text carries the message.

Of course we have no survey data from the crucial years of the Loyalist immigration. (Pity, eh?) But a careful historian or social scientist can tell us much. Thus, Kenneth McRae concludes that the Loyalists were American liberals. "As the central figure of the English-Canadian tradition we encounter once again the American liberal." See McRae, "The Structure of Canadian History," in Louis Hartz et al., *The Founding of New Societies* (1964). McRae's conclusion is the more striking because he agrees with many of Gad Horowitz' suppositions about the march of political ideologies and the importance of culture. The difference is this: McRae combed the documentary evidence.

The Marxian model, the notion of a necessary progression

Sources 153

from right to left, treats liberalism as one ideology among others. If we adopt Locke rather than Marx, we will see liberalism as a philosophy of constitutionalism allowing the free play of opinions, arguments, and ideologies. "Liberalism" becomes, not one of the ideologies, but a way of managing the *contestation* of ideologies. Are Canadian Lockeans? Over the years Parliament has seen a surprising range of political opinions. Consider the joke about the Canadian Parliament in the 1990s. One major opposition party (the Reform Party) had serious doubts about the legitimacy of Parliament while another (the Bloc Québécois) had serious doubts about the legitimacy of Canada. Talk about Lockean tolerance! (But though we may have a Lockean Parliament we continue to try to understand it by means of a Marxian model.)

Isaiah Berlin is sometimes described as the foremost political thinker of our time to defend the Enlightenment and liberal democracy. But, as commentators note, he wrote more about the Counter-Enlightenment than about the liberal philosophers and he had a sneaking admiration for the romantics. His fascination with them, his sheer enjoyment of their thought – profound, soaring, rebellious, absurd – is surely nowhere more evident than in *The Roots of Romanticism*.

The lectures reproduced in *The Roots of Romanticism* were given in 1965 as the A.W. Mellon Lectures in the Fine Arts at the National Gallery of Art in Washington, D.C. They were broadcasted by the BBC on several occasions but were prepared for publication only after Berlin's death in 1997. See Berlin, *The Roots of Romanticism* (Princeton, N.J.: Princeton University Press 1999).

For an interesting conversation about Berlin's thought on the Counter-Enlightenment, see Mark Lilla, Ronald Dworkin and Robert Silvers, ed., *The Legacy of Isaiah Berlin* (New York: New York Review of Books 2001). Among the contributors are Avishai Margalit, Thomas Nagel, Charles Taylor, Michael Walzer, and Bernard Williams.

I do not attempt a comparison of Judith Shklar and Isaiah Berlin. Is she more pessimistic? Perhaps. She is no less convinced that the study of romanticism is crucial to the understanding of modern political thought. See Judith Shklar, *After Utopia: The Decline of Political Faith* (Princeton, N.J.: Princeton University Press 1957).

CHAPTER TWO

A Compas poll of April 2002 found that a large number of Canadians are confused about the difference between "right" and "left" in politics. Only 47 per cent put the Canadian Alliance party to the right of the New Democratic Party (NDP); 18 per cent put the Alliance to the left of the NDP. See *National Post*, 29 April 2002, A1. Are Canadians just ignorant? Fed up with politics? I don't think so. The trouble lies with the model: right-centre-left.

Canadians often use "conservative" to describe what in this book I call a liberal, especially when the liberal has a strong sense of prudence. Here's a beautiful formulation of someone whom I would call "liberal" but whom the author describes as a conservative:

... the true conservative listens deeply to the lessons of history as he strives to protect enduring political, moral, and social institutions. He is moved by "the voice of the people," of course, but in a far different way from the radical. He is attuned, to borrow G.K. Chesterton's fine phrase, to "the democracy of the dead ..." Namely, all that has been thought, felt, and passed down to us, that lives on in the concrete forms, customs, habits, principles, and symbols of the best of our ancestors. When the conservative acts to change a thing, it is with the knowledge that circumstances will soon alter yet again. So he must change with prudence, not merely for his own time, but with due respect for the future generations to which he feels we must all be responsible.

The author is William D. Gairdner, in the introduction to Gairdner, ed., *After Liberalism: Essays in Search of Freedom, Virtue, and Order* (Toronto: Stoddart 1998). It's a major flaw of the right-centre-left model that it has no place for someone of this description, call her "conservative," call her "liberal."

Who gets what? The phrase comes from Harold Lasswell's *Politics: Who Gets What, When, How* (New York: Peter Smith 1950; first published in 1936). People continue to use it as a definition of politics, but no one's ever completely happy with it.

In 1990–91 Keith Spicer chaired a highly publicized commission of inquiry into Canadians' views on constitutional reform and the constitutional process. The result was *Citizens' Forum on*

Sources

Canada's Future: Report to the People and Government of Canada (the Spicer Report) (Ottawa: Supply and Services 1991). Polls showing discontent with politicians and politics are numerous. It would be easy to conclude that Canadians are an angry, anxious bunch. But, curiously, when pollsters ask whether they're happy, most Canadians say they are. And why not? They have a good life. Canada shows up well in comparisons with European countries on "quality of life" and "citizen satisfaction" measures.

That one realizes oneself fully in and through "community" is a typically romantic contention. The doubtful liberal may object: aren't communities sometimes oppressive, stifling individual freedoms? Isn't one's family sometimes oppressive, for that matter? Well possibly, the romantic might reply, but if we had a new concept of democracy, a new idea of citizenship, the tension would resolve itself. The back cover of Irshad Manji's delightful and informative *Risking Utopia* states boldly: "Manji unveils new ways for people to assert their individuality while building community." See *Risking Utopia: On the Edge of a New Democracy* (Toronto: Douglas and McIntyre 1997). And note *this* statement, again from the back cover: "[Manji] convincingly suggests the need to move beyond all-too-common-sense notions of left and right in favour of the messiness – sometimes painful, often joyful – of a life beyond categories."

For the importance of new politics in Canada, see Neil Nevitte and Roger Gibbins, *New Elites in Old Societies: Ideologies in the Anglo-American Democracies* (Toronto: Oxford University Press 1990). A helpful short article on the subject is Nevitte's "New Politics," in Mark O. Dickerson, Thomas Flanagan and Neil Nevitte, ed., *Introductory Readings in Government and Politics*, 3rd ed. (Scarborough, Ont.: Nelson Canada 1991). Nevitte is drawing on the observations of Ronald Inglehart.

Would changing the electoral system remedy "cabinet oligarchy"? The jury is out. According to some scholars, electoral reform that relies on a party "list" would indeed give us a House of Commons that more closely mirrored voters' choices; but it would also enhance the power of party leaders, thus strengthening cabinet oligarchy.

I can't list all reforms to the political process in vogue today.

Canadians' gift for invention flourishes in this area. A place to start might be Judy Rebick, *Imagine Democracy* (Toronto: Stoddart 2000). Rebick argues in lively fashion for radical reform of the Canadian political process, illustrating her contentions with references to recent Canadian controversies. She describes herself as a radical socialist and feminist. Where does she fit in the liberal-romantic scheme? She thinks in terms of rational categories like a woman of the Enlightenment, and in this sense she's a liberal. Of sorts. According to Irshad Manji, Rebick is far too ready to rely on categories and "the canon of absolutes." She doesn't listen and doesn't acknowledge different perspectives (*Risking Utopia*, 17). The romantic embraces her objectives but finds her mode of argument offensively "liberal."

Another helpful book is Peter Russell, ed., *The Future of Social Democracy: Views of Leaders from around the World* (Toronto: University of Toronto Press 1999). Few of the social democrats in this volume advocate radical reforms to the political process of the kind Rebick desires.

"What's wanted is 'a process that not only hears all voices but takes all experiences and aspirations into account.'" In the debates leading to the national referendum of 1992 many academics and lobbyists made pronouncements like this. The author in this instance is Donna Greschner. See her "Commentary," in David E. Smith, Peter MacKinnon, and John C. Courtney, ed. *After Meech Lake: Lessons for the Future* (Saskatoon, Sask.: Fifth House 1991), 224. Chapter 14 below takes up issues in these national debates and offers more examples of the argument for consensus.

It's usual to describe "Peace, Order, and Good Government" as a "conservative" prescription, emphasizing communal values and the public good. "Life, liberty and the pursuit of happiness" supposedly emphasizes liberal individualism. Thus it's said that conservative Canada has POGG, while the liberal United States has "life and liberty." That's the difference between the two political societies. Well, dear friends, I'm afraid that I can't see the difference. Without institutions that promote civil peace, there's no security for life and liberty. And when you have a constitution that guarantees life and liberty, you have peace, order, and good government. "Life and liberty" is a phrase dear to John Locke and thus comes into the British and Canadian political traditions from early days.

Sources 157

CHAPTER THREE

Doris Lessing describes our tendency to forget and deny the state murders of the twentieth century in *The Wind Blows Away Our Words, and Other Documents relating to the Afghan Resistance* (London: Pan Books 1987). Recent commentators put the toll at one hundred and twenty-five million.

In November 2000 forensic anthropologist Owen Beattie spoke at McMaster University about his experiences in Rwanda as a member of an international team of forensic observers. In that unfortunate country, perhaps 800,000 people had been slaughtered in just one hundred days. But the exact number will never be known. The bodies were sealed in mass graves in jumbled heaps, or scattered in mineshafts and the corners of fields. There are no records, no death certificates. There is no tally. There are no names. Beattie is appalled at the slaughter, as I do not need to say. He is also deeply disturbed by the lack of records. He saw heaps of bodies but was not allowed to count and identify. In orderly societies, especially in liberal democracies, everyone who dies must be identified. In Rwanda, people were thrown away like refuse.

How far some romantics will go to defend state terror is suggested by this poem exonerating the Cheka, the secret police of the USSR. The poet is Hugh MacDiarmid, and I take the verse from an essay on MacDiarmid by Seamus Heaney in *The Redress of Poetry* (London: Faber and Faber 1995): "As necessary, and insignificant, as death/ Wi' a' its agonies in the cosmos still/ The Cheka's horrors are in their degree;/ And'll end suner! What maitters't wha we kill/ To lessen that foulest murder that deprives/ Maist men o' real lives?"

For a defence of the extreme forms of romantic democracy, see C.B. Macpherson, *The Real World of Democracy* ([Toronto]: Canadian Broadcasting Corporation 1965) and *The Life and Times of Liberal Democracy* (Oxford, U.K.: Oxford University Press 1977). Macpherson believed Canadian liberal democracy demonstrably inferior to forms of strong democracy developing in the (then) Soviet Union and in Africa. It's an extraordinary thing that all his life one of Canada's most respected political scientists and thinkers defended Soviet and African totalitarianism. Judy Rebick acknowledges his influence. "Macpherson suggested we could expand our own ideas of democracy by learning from various societies in the developing world. Instead we have brutally imposed our ideas about economics and how society should work on them." See Rebick, *Imagine Democracy* (Toronto: Stoddart 2000), 49. A book that incorporates an assessment of Macpherson while defending parliamentary liberal democracy is Douglas V. Verney, *The Analysis of Political Systems* (Glencoe, Ill.: Free Press 1959).

The idea that tyranny follows democracy is a familiar theme in political philosophy. In Book Eight of *The Republic*, Plato describes a happy-go-lucky regime called "democracy" which falls into warring factions in part because no one pays enough attention to the business of politics. When the quarrelling threatens to destroy all pleasure and freedom, a tyrant arises and promises to unite the regime. Exhausted and frightened, the populace says, "Welcome, sir," and so they give up their remaining liberty and become slaves.

Hobbes offers a similar picture in *Leviathan* (1651). The absolute monarch comes to his throne with the promise to end the war of each man against each man. In Hobbes's sour version, despotism of this kind is humanity's only hope.

Berlin discusses fascism as an "inheritor" of the romantic movement in *The Roots of Romanticism* (Princeton, N.J.: Princeton University Press 1999) 145, and elsewhere. But see page 134, where he argues that "romanticism [appears] on the surface to say everything and its opposite." At one time it argues for extreme individualism and at another, for the inevitability of community. Judith Shklar develops the idea that totalitarianism represents the "degeneracy" of romanticism in a number of places. See especially *After Utopia: The Decline of Political Faith* (Princeton, N.J.: Princeton University Press 1957), 106–7.

For Locke on the dangers of religious enthusiasm and on the separation of church and state, see *A Letter Concerning Toleration*, first published in 1869. It's sometimes argued that Canada does not adhere to the Lockean teaching on church and state since we allow public funding or tax relief for schools associated with particular religions or denominations. Supposedly, the United States follows Locke and we do not. But Locke did not intend a firewall. What's important is that religious affiliation should not legitimate institutions of hierarchy and dominance. Canada and

Britain as much as the United States exemplify Locke's teaching on church and state.

"Here we encounter a difficulty." Judith Shklar sums it up: "Liberalism is a political philosophy, romanticism a *Weltanschauung*, a state of mind which can adapt itself to the most divergent types of political thought" (*After Utopia*, 231).

Souls without Longing is the title Allan Bloom first proposed for the book that became *The Closing of the American Mind* (New York: Simon and Schuster 1987). The students at American universities have no longing for the good. They are deficient because they lack the true romantic sentiment. That was Bloom's thesis. Allan Bloom, the notorious American right-winger, the some-time defender of American liberal democracy, had a romantic heart! (But did you ever doubt it?)

Think of Leonard Cohen's song, "Death of a Ladies Man": "the art of longing's over and it's never coming back." Think, too, of "McWorld." The term refers to global capitalism. You pronounce it with a sneer. See Benjamin R. Barber, *Jihad vs. McWorld* (New York: Ballantine 1995). Barber argues that the central conflict of our times is the opposition between consumerist capitalism and religious fundamentalism. The book is dedicated to Judith Shklar, but Barber has moved far from her model. He sees the West through the eyes of the Counter-Enlightenment; liberalism's faith in political science and reason was never anything but a faint hope – or a lie.

For a highly romantic tirade about the bleakness of modern life, see the British conservative Roger Scruton in *The West and the Rest: Globalization and the Terrorist Threat* (Wilmington, Del.: Intercollegiate Studies 2002). A review of this work notes: "Western society, Mr. Scruton contends, has become bleakly contractual. The ideals of the Enlightenment have been perverted, resulting in a destruction of community and a 'culture of negation.' Westerners pray not to God but worship instead the Moloch of consumerism. The West's loyalty to the nation-state is attenuated by immigration, multiculturalism and by globalism, which in turn, breeds vipers in its own bosom and foists on Islam what it so scathingly derides as the 'Great Satan'" (Kevin Michael Grace, *The Report*, 23 September 2002, 59).

Why do I say that liberals are optimists and romantics are pessimists? Liberals don't expect much from human nature, and so they're often pleased with moderate successes. They begin as pessimists and end as optimists. Romantics begin as optimists and end as pessimists. Their vaulting hopes for individual and communal perfection are seldom satisfied.

Is liberalism more likely to lead to totalitarianism? Michael Sandel sums up the quarrel between liberals and romantic communitarians in the introduction to his edited collection *Liberalism and Its Critics* (New York: New York University Press 1984), 7: the liberal says that "any attempt to govern by a vision of the good is likely to lead to a slippery slope of totalitarian temptations. Communitarians reply that intolerance flourishes most where forms of life are dislocated, roots unsettled, traditions undone. In our day, the totalitarian impulse has sprung less from convictions of confidently situated selves than from the confusions of atomized, dislocated, frustrated selves, at sea in a world where common meanings have lost their force."

When does romanticism come on the scene? Berlin suggests that the date of the French Revolution is appropriate. Others, like Kenneth Clark, maintain that romanticism is a perennial impulse of the human heart. According to Clark, some people are born to the tradition of romanticism in every age, and some are born to classicism.

On the importance of 1688, I recommend Edmund S. Morgan, *Inventing the People: The Rise of Popular Sovereignty in England and America* (New York: W.W. Norton 1988). Morgan says nothing about Canada, of course. Canada seldom figures on the world map of political ideas.

A good source for the documents of Canada's early history is W.P.M. Kennedy, *Statutes, Treaties and Documents of the Canadian Constitution, 1713–1929* (Toronto: Oxford University Press 1930). It's out of print but available in university and legislative libraries or, if you're lucky, from an antiquarian bookseller.

CHAPTER FOUR

My account of the demonstration by the Ontario Coalition Against Poverty is drawn from a story by Christie Blatchford in the *National Post*, 17 October 2001, A1.

Robert Frost's "Nothing Gold Can Stay" appeared in 1923.

> Nature's first green is gold,
> Her hardest hue to hold.
> Her early leaf's a flower;
> But only so an hour.
> Then leaf subsides to leaf,
> So Eden sank to grief,
> So dawn goes down to day.
> Nothing gold can stay.

"Romantic hearts beat high." A famous passage in "The Prelude" (1900) expresses Wordsworth's hopes for the French Revolution:

> Bliss was it in that dawn to be alive,
> But to be young was very Heaven! O times,
> In which the meagre, stale, forbidding ways
> Of custom, law, and statute, took at once
> The attraction of a country in romance!

"Dark and more dark the shades of evening fell." Wordworth's "Composed After a Journey" (probably from 1802) describes a journey through the English countryside; we know that the romantic poets felt despair at the decline of the French Revolution into violence and tyranny but I have to admit that this is not a poem embodying that despair. Compare Lord Byron in "Childe Harold's Pilgrimage" (1818): "But France got drunk with blood to vomit crime/And fatal have her Saturnalia been/To Freedom's cause ..."

For Pierre Bédard's story, see N-E Dionne, *Pierre Bédard et ses fils* (Quebec City: Laflamme et Proulx 1909), and Janet Ajzenstat "Canada's First Constitution: Pierre Bédard on Tolerance and Dissent," *Canadian Journal of Political Science* 23:1 (March 1990).

According to Fernand Ouellet, Louis-Joseph Papineau was a "divided soul" because he continued to enjoy the life of a feudal seignieur in Lower Canada while advocating democratic reform. In private life he looked back to French Canadian traditions that were already passing out of existence. In politics he looked to the future. See Fernand Ouellet, *Louis-Joseph Papineau: A Divided Soul*, translated by Douglas Wurtele (Ottawa: Canadian Historical Association 1968).

I am less certain than Ouellet that there is a contradiction between tradition and romantic democracy. It's true that romantics are often scornful of tradition's constraints. But many profess admiration for the simple life where nothing much changes from generation to generation, and the argument is often that in such a community democracy flourishes. In the preface to the Second Discourse (*The Discourse on the Origin and Foundations of Inequality among Men*), Rousseau praises the stupifyingly traditional life of the artisans and farmers in the republic of Geneva, and notes especially its democratic character. (The *Discourse* was published in 1775; it's doubtful that Geneva had the features that Rousseau ascribes to it. But it's the thought that counts, eh?) Did Papineau read Rousseau? Of course. Was Quebec in the first decades of the nineteenth century just such a Rousseauistic democracy? Perhaps. More than one observer has thought so.

According to Rousseau, equality of material condition was an essential part of the democratic formula. We know that the seignieurs of Quebec were not markedly wealthier than their tenants. The province had the outward forms of a feudal society but not the sharp differences of wealth and class. Clever (male) youngsters of every rank could obtain a good education. Birth was not an impediment to political ambition. Lord Durham remarks on the phenomenon with surprise. See Janet Ajzenstat, *The Political Thought of Lord Durham* (Montreal: McGill-Queen's University Press 1988), 89–90. In short, many of the elements of Rousseau's democratic prescription were present in Quebec: material equality, a strong sense of tradition, and sturdy agrarian self-sufficiency.

On the Canadian radicals and romantics of the 1830s, see Louis-Georges Harvey, "The First Distinct Society: French Canada, America, and the Constitution of 1791," in Janet Ajzenstat and Peter J. Smith ed., *Canada's Origins: Liberal, Tory or Republican* (Ottawa: Carleton University Press 1995), Chapter 4. Harvey agrees with Peter Smith that the revolutionaries of 1837–8 were civic humanists (civic republicans). His article concludes: the civic humanists "could no more compromise with [liberal] constitutionalism than they could with the devil." The entire article is singularly rewarding.

Robert Hollinger defends the idea that democracy must always be in play in *The Dark Side of Liberalism: Elitism vs. Democracy* (Westport, Conn.: Praeger 1996). For a dyed-in-the wool Canadian romantic of the anti-institutional kind, consider Rick Salutin. "For all Salutin's activism, he was never inclined toward party politics. 'Parties just seemed ludicrous to me,' he says. 'Politics was about revolution and class conflict – it wasn't about hammering up lawn signs! The party structures themselves are just not worth putting allegiance into'" (Rachel Pulfer, "The Antagonist," *Toronto Life*, September 2002).

Hope springs eternal. We have Lord Byron's assurance in "Childe Harolde's Pilgrimage":

... the sap lasts, – and still the seed we find
Sown deep, even in the bosom of the North,
So shall a better spring less bitter fruit bring forth.

CHAPTER FIVE

For a sympathetic view of the Family Compacts, see the essays by S.F. Wise in *God's Peculiar People: Essays on Political Culture in Nineteenth Century Canada*, ed. A.B. McKillop and Paul Romney (Ottawa: Carleton University Press 1993).

In 1836 Robert Baldwin made the case for responsible government in a letter to the colonial secretary, Lord Glenelg. Excerpts from it can be found in H.D. Forbes, ed., *Canadian Political Thought* (Toronto: Oxford University Press 1985), 26–33. Forbes's volume is an invaluable source of primary documents. For this chapter, see the section entitled "Canadian Voices of Reform and Revolt." In addition to Baldwin's letter it contains statements by Papineau and Mackenzie, in brief form.

See also see Joseph Howe's four public letters to Lord John Russell in support of Lord Durham on responsible government, in W.P.M. Kennedy, ed., *Statutes, Treaties, and Documents of the Canadian Constitution* (Toronto: Oxford University Press 1930), cvi–cix.

Christopher Moore argues that Conservatives were slower than the Liberals to accept responsible government. Very likely. After all, some of those Conservatives had benefited from the old oligarchic system. But in the end they did accept parliamentary government, proving that they were at heart adherents of the liberal ideology as I am describing it. By the time of the Confederation debates, they were as staunch as the Liberals in defending parliamentary institutions. See Christopher Moore, *1867: How the Fathers Made a Deal* (Toronto: McClelland and Stewart 1997).

"There's a sense that the power is going the wrong way." Bill Blaikie's statement on the problems of responsible government appears in an article by Sheldon Alberts in the *National Post*, 12 February 2001, page A2. The *Post* ran a useful series on reform of Parliament from the 12th to the 17th. It is no surprise to find that the "right" and "left" are of one mind about the need for reform. Preston Manning of the Alliance Party expressed his agreement with Blaikie, who sits for the New Democrats: "I think the backbenchers are just grossly underused." This is not the place to discuss proposals for reform of Parliament. I will say only that they fall into two categories. In the first are reforms like the referendum, initiative, and recall that cannot be reconciled with parliamentary liberal democracy in its classic form. In the second are reforms that would roll back twentieth-century attempts to "improve" the system. Thus, Christopher Moore recommends "the heave." Members of a party's parliamentary caucus were once able to give their party leader the heave-ho. (Today the party membership elects leaders at a party convention.) I'll leave it to readers to work out the ramifications of the two systems. Which system is preferable if our objective is to curb the autocratic ambitions of prime ministers and cabinet? Election at a convention appears more democratic. But is it? In a similar vein is the suggestion that riding organizations have the last say in nomination of political candidates. They once had it but now party leaders have a veto. The idea is to choose reforms that are in keeping with classical parliamentary democracy and past practice. Turn back the clock? Why not? The future may not hold all the remedies.

Even before the introduction of responsible government, thoughtful colonists were concerned that the principle might lend too much strength to the executive branch, thus reducing opportunities for effective political opposition in the Commons. Jeffrey L. McNairn discusses the issue and refers readers to documents in *Capacity to Judge: Public Opinion and Deliberative Democracy in Upper Canada, 1791 to 1854* (Toronto: University of Toronto Press 2000).

A great authority on politics and parliamentary deliberation is Bernard Crick, *In Defence of Politics* (Chicago: University of Chicago Press, revised edition, 1972).

CHAPTER SIX

For Lord Durham's definition of responsible government, see the Carleton Library edition (*Lord Durham's Report*, edited and with an introduction by Gerald M. Craig [Toronto: McClelland and Stewart 1963], 56. The passage begins with this description of the oligarchy in Lower Canada (the Chateau Clique): "Fortified by family connexion, and the common interest felt by all who held, and all who desired, subordinate offices, [the ruling party] was ... erected into a solid and permanent power, controlled by no responsibility, subject to no serious change, exercising over the whole of the Province an authority utterly independent of the people and its representatives, and possessing the only means of influencing either the Government at home, or the colonial representative of the Crown."

Durham doesn't ascribe the desire for political office and power to sinister motives. He regards political ambition as the "natural" attribute of political men. The passage continues: "This entire separation of the legislative and executive powers of a State, is the natural error of governments desirous of being free from the check of representative institutions. Since the Revolution of 1688, the stability of the English Constitution has been secured ..." The *Report* was first published in 1839. The best complete edition is C.P. Lucas, ed., *Lord Durham's Report on the Affairs of British North America* (Oxford: Clarendon Press 1912, 3 vols.). The third volume includes appendixes on various aspects of politics and life in the colonies, some by Durham's radical friends.

Aileen Dunham was perhaps the first historian to argue that the British had barely developed an understanding of responsible government before Durham described it. See Dunham *Political Unrest in Upper Canada, 1815–1836* (Toronto: McClelland and Stewart [Carleton Library] 1963; first published in 1927). In 1976 J.M. Ward was still suggesting that "responsible government in the modern sense" did not become "a convention of the [British] constitution until the 1840s." See Ward, *Colonial Self-Government: The British Experience in 1759–1856* (London: Macmillan 1976), 172 (cited in Phillip Buckner, *The Transition to Responsible Government: British Policy in British North America, 1815–1850* [Westport, Conn.: Greenwood 1985], 5). Buckner tells the story of the historians' muddle on pages 4 and 5.

A charmingly wrongheaded "historical minute" filmed by the Bronfman Foundation for television, focuses on the reaction of the young Queen Victoria to news of the wonderful Canadian invention, responsible government. She grasps the point immediately. Executive officers must have the support of the people's elected representatives in the popular house. "Only in Canada?" she says thoughtfully. "Pity!"

Durham visited the radical John Arthur Roebuck before he left for British North America, and Roebuck gave him a blistering summary of radical opinion on the colonial debacle. It was later published in Roebuck's *The Colonies of England: A Plan for the Government of Some Portion of Our Colonial Possessions* (London: John W. Parker 1849). For more on Roebuck and the British philosophical radicals, see Janet Ajzenstat, *The Political Thought of Lord Durham* (Kingston: McGill Queen's Press 1988), Chapter 6. Roebuck was paid by the Legislative Assembly of Lower Canada to represent them in the British Parliament and, like any good representative or lawyer, reported back to his clients on a regular basis. These reports and his letters to assembly leader Louis-Joseph Papineau are available in Canada's Public Archives. Though Papineau and Roebuck saw eye to eye on political matters, they differed on the question of nationality. Roebuck had no appreciation whatsoever for the national feelings of the French Canadians. (But Papineau said nothing on the record to suggest lack confidence in his agent.) Janet Ajzenstat, "Collectivity and Individual Right in 'Mainstream' Liberalism: John Arthur Roebuck and the *Patriotes*," *Journal of Canadian Studies* 19:3 (fall 1984).

Did Durham understand the American constitution? Did he think it was a liberal constitution? It's not clear. It may be that he relied too much on the radical interpretation. All the radicals of the period, British and colonial, regarded the United States as a highly democratic country – democratic in the republican, romantic definition. See Louis-Georges Harvey, "The First Distinct Society: French Canada, America and the Constitution of 1791," in Janet Ajzenstat, ed., *Canadian Constitutionalism, 1791–1991* (Ottawa: Canadian Study of Parliament Group 1992).

The Rule of Law: In a folk song from the 1960s the singer bemoans the travails of her noble lover, caught poaching in the king's forest: "Oh-h Geordie will be hanged in a gold-e-en chain/ T'is not the chain of m-a-any." The penalty for shooting the king's deer was death. Geordie will pay in full, like any other poacher, rich or poor, high or low. But as a concession to his aristocratic rank, he will not be strung up with plebeian rope.

"At Canada's founding, its people were not sovereign, and there was not even a sense that a constituent sovereign people would have to be invented." See Peter H, Russell, *Constitutional Odyssey: Can Canadians Be a Sovereign People?* (Toronto: University of Toronto Press 1992). See also Reg Whitaker, *A Sovereign Idea: Essays on Canada as a Democratic Community* (Montreal McGill-Queen's University Press 1992), and Philip Resnick, *Parliament vs. People: An Essay on Democracy and Canadian Political Culture* (Vancouver: Star Books 1984). Indeed it's been said that the Canadian Fathers ignored all philosophical doctrines. "It is well known that the Fathers of Confederation were pragmatic lawyers for the most part, more given to fine tuning the details of a constitutional act than to waxing philosophical about human rights or national goals." Ramsay Cook, "Canada 200: Towards a Post-Nationalist Canada," *Cité Libre* (fall 2000), 82.

"All ran to meet their chains." See Rousseau's Second Discourse (*Discourse on the Origins and Foundations of Inequality among Men*), second part.

On romanticism and democracy, see William D. Gairdner, *The Trouble with Democracy: A Citizen speaks Out* (Toronto: Stoddart 2001), especially 183–94. The section begins: "Political theorists have paid too little attention to the role of literature and the arts in the shaping of modern political ideals, and this is especially true of Rousseau's period." The entire book is helpful.

Quotations from the Confederation debates in the colonial legislatures are taken from Janet Ajzenstat, Paul Romney, Ian Gentles, and William D. Gairdner, ed., *Canada's Founding Debates* (Toronto: Stoddart 1999; reissued by University of Toronto Press 2003), especially chapters 11 and 12. The excerpts in *Canada's Founding Debates* are presented thematically. To locate particular quotations, readers should use the volume's index of names and subjects.

"The rule was simple. The local parliaments and assemblies

had a veto." See G.P. Browne, ed., *Documents on the Confederation of British North America* (Toronto: McClelland and Stewart 1969). In a sense the provincial parliaments were "in the loop" from the beginning of the constitutional process. Delegates arrived at Charlottetown with authorization from their provincial parliaments to discuss union in some form or other. See Browne, *Documents*, 24, 25.

When did the inhabitants of the Thirteen Colonies become one "people"? For Edmund Morgan's answer, see *Inventing the People: The Rise of Popular Sovereignty in England and America* (New York: W.W. Norton 1988), Chapter 11.

"It has long been known that the Fathers of Confederation were not democrats": Phillip Buckner, "The Maritimes and Confederation: A Reassessment," *Canadian Historical Review* 81:1 (1990), 1–30, 23. To be fair to Buckner, it has to be said that his article was not written to explore issues of democracy. It was intended to show that the Confederation literature exaggerates the degree of Maritime opposition to Confederation. Christopher Moore argues that the picture of the Fathers as anti-democrats has been standard from sometime in the 1960s. See Moore, *1867: How the Fathers Made a Deal* (Toronto: McClelland and Stewart 1997), 106, 122–3, 196, and elsewhere.

CHAPTER SEVEN

Everyone who's seen the play or the movie *The Madness of King George* will be amused by the idea that at the end of the eighteenth century the British monarch was neutral vis-à-vis the parties. The play makes no bones about George the Third's decided preference for Pitt over Fox. But it also suggests that constitutional principles tugged at the national conscience and that even the king knew the crown *ought* to be impartial.

For the Fathers' views on responsible government, see Janet Ajzenstat, Paul Romney, Ian Gentles, and William D. Gairdner, ed., *Canada's Founding Debates* (Toronto: Stoddart 1999; reissued by University of Toronto Press 2003), chapters 1 and 2. For their views on the accumulation of wealth, see chapter 5.

"It has long been known that the Fathers of Confederation were not democrats": Phillip Buckner, "The Maritimes and Confederation: A Reassessment," *Canadian Historical Review* 81:1

(190), 1–30, 23. See also Hernando de Soto, *The Mystery of Capital: Why Capitalism Triumphs in the West and Fails Everywhere Else* (New York: Basic Books 2000).

Undoubtedly Buckner wants a larger lower house because he wishes to see it broadly representative. Limiting the size of the lower house might restrict representation. I would never deny that broad representation is desirable. We should be glad that today's Commons is more representative of our population than the Commons of 1867. We should be glad we have a broader franchise. Yet I suggest that the crucial factors in parliamentary systems are the separation of powers and responsible government. A system with separation of powers and *restricted* franchise and representation (restricted to men, for example; or limited by a property qualification) still offers the advantages of liberal democracy (although we may wish for reforms). Where you have responsible government and a restricted franchise, you still have competition for the rewards of office and thus for support of house and electorate. What usually happens, in good time, is that one party and then another finds it to its advantage to introduce an extension of the franchise and to seek out candidates from a variety of backgrounds.

The monarch has the power but does not wield it. Another way to put this point is to say that in our parliamentary system the governor general is head of state while the prime minister is head of government. It bothered the Canadian founders that the American president is both head of state and head of government. The arrangement seemed to them too "democratic." If the person representing the state and the constitution had been put in place by a popular majority, the position of the political opposition would not be secure. Over the years, the friends of parliamentary government repeated this argument many times. But to be fair to the Americans, it has to be said that in practice everything seems to work out for them. The president wears his two hats more or less comfortably and usually remembers when he is speaking as head of state for all the people and for the country as a whole, and when he is speaking as head of government, on behalf of a party with a contestable program and elected by a temporary majority.

In the spring of 2002, the auditor general of Canada accused the Liberal Party government of hiving off great sums of money in special accounts in order to escape scrutiny by the House of Commons. Such accusations have become an annual occurrence. The old contest between the government and the House of Commons continues. We should listen to the auditor general!

CHAPTER EIGHT

For quotations from the legislative debates, see Janet Ajzenstat, Paul Romney, Ian Gentles, and William D. Gairdner, ed., *Canada's Founding Debates* (Toronto: Stoddart 1999; reissued by University of Toronto Press 2003).

Cartier is less friendly towards the American constitution than John A. Macdonald because he relies on the interpretation of U.S. institutions promulgated by the romantics of 1837. The romantics believed that the United States was the home of strong democracy. Their heroes were Jefferson and Jackson. Did they exaggerate the romantic character of the American constitution? So I would argue. Yet it remains true that Cartier has adopted their picture. They admire "democracy" in this definition. He deplores it.

Macdonald, in contrast, sees the United States as a system of checks and balances, very like British parliamentary government. Here he is in the Confederation debates in the Canadian Legislative Assembly (1865): "It is the fashion now to enlarge on the defects of the constitution of the United States, but I am not one of those who look upon it as a failure. I think and believe that it is one of the most skilful works which human intelligence ever created; it is one of the most perfect organizations that ever governed a free people. To say that it has some defects is but to say that it is not the work of Omniscience, but of human intellects." I don't mean to say Macdonald thought the American constitution perfect in all respects; he had a few improvements up his sleeve.

To put the arguments of Macdonald and Cartier in perspective, here's a statement by an able opponent, A.-A. Dorion, heir of the *patriote's* romantic philosophy:

It is but natural that ...[the] honourable gentlemen opposite want to keep as much power as possible in the hands of the government – that is the doctrine of the Conservative Party everywhere – that is the line which distinguishes the Tories from the Whigs – the Tories always side with the crown, and the Liberals always want to give more power and influence to the people. The instincts of honourable gentlemen opposite, whether you take the Honourable Attorney General East [Cartier] or the Honourable Attorney General West [John A. Macdonald], lead them to this – they think the hands of the crown should be strengthened and the influence of the people, if possible, diminished. (Canadian Legislative Assembly, 1865).

Scholars often argue that Conservatives in 1867 favoured a strong central government in the federation. Indeed, it's sometimes suggested that all the Fathers without exception were centralists. Thus, it's said that the British Judicial Committee of the Privy Council (which until 1949 was the final court of appeal for the colonies and the Dominion of Canada on questions of federalism) favoured the provinces unduly, strengthening provincial powers under the British North America Act and shrinking federal powers until the original intent of the Fathers was turned on its head. This interpretation of the Confederation period and the jurisprudence of the Judicial Committee is debunked by Robert C. Vipond, and Paul Romney. It's not correct to suppose that all the Conservatives who participated in the drafting of the British North America Act, 1867 were centralists. Cartier, for one, always kept his eye out for the welfare of Quebec. And, as I suggested above, one shouldn't discount provincial-rights Liberals like George Brown and Oliver Mowat, or, for that matter, the stalwart defenders of local institutions in the Maritimes! The better view maintains that the Fathers intended the BNA Act to balance an effective general government with secure powers for the provinces. The Judicial Committee's interpretations are an attempt to respect that balance. See Paul Romney, *Getting It Wrong: How Canadians Forgot Their Past and Imperilled Confederation* (Toronto: University of Toronto Press 1999), and Robert C. Vipond, *Canadian Federalism and the Failure of the Constitution* (Albany, N.Y.: State University of New York Press 1991). Vipond and Romney have not persuaded all scholars. In *The Lawmakers: Judicial Power and the Shaping of Canadian Federalism* (Toronto: University of Toronto Press/Osgoode Society for Canadian Legal History 2002), John T. Saywell turns the tables again, defending the traditional view that the Judicial Committee ignored the Fathers' intentions.

Christopher Moore alerts us to the importance of the capital-L

Liberals in the drafting of the British North America Act (now the Constitution Act, 1867) in *1867: How the Fathers Made a Deal* (Toronto: McClelland and Stewart 1997). The classic guide to scholarly opinion on the Judicial Committee is Alan Cairn's "The Judicial Committee and Its Critics," in Douglas E. Williams, ed., *Constitution, Government, and Society in Canada: Selected Essays by Alan C. Cairns* (Toronto: McClelland and Stewart 1988).

On Canadian mixed government, see Philip Resnick, "Montesquieu Revisited, or the Mixed Constitution and the Separation of Powers," *Canadian Journal of Political Science* 20 (1987), and the replies to Resnick by Janet Ajzenstat and Rod Preece in the same issue. See also Janet Ajzenstat, "Modern Mixed Government: A Liberal Defence of Inequality," *Canadian Journal of Political Science* 18:1 (1985).

There's a story in Jean-Louis de Lolme's *The Constitution of England* (1776) to illustrate the idea of equality in English law. De Lolme, newly come from Geneva to study the famous English tradition of rights, is rattling up from the coast on his way to the city of London. For endless miles the carriage rolls by a forest confined by a wall. At last de Lolme sees a gate with a notice on it: "trespassers will be prosecuted." He asks whose forest it is and his companions tell him that it is the king's. De Lolme calls for the horses to stop, gets out of the carriage, and kisses the ground. This is English freedom! This is English equality. This is the rule of law. Even the king may not charge a trespasser without due process of law. He can't drop the offender down an oubliette. His complaint must be proved under law.

"Natural kings." Was Trudeau one? Undoubtedly. And he would surely have preferred to rule without the Commons. It's amazing that the fragile parliamentary system curbs these natural kings and tyrants. (But I can hear critics grumbling that it sometimes works too slowly.)

In the eighteenth century and until some point in the nineteenth, it was argued that the "three branches" represented the "estates" or classes of English history. But the original connection between the social estates and representation in the branches of Parliament had begun to wear away even before the Glorious Revolution of 1688. The Constitutional Act of 1791 (the act that established representative government in Upper and Lower Canada) permitted creation of a provincial nobility whose members could demand a writ of summons to the upper house. But the permission was not acted on, and in the Confederation debates of the 1860s no one proposed a comparable measure. There was to be no "lordly" estate in the Dominion of Canada.

Excerpts from the speeches of Brown and Macdonald on the mode of selecting Senators for the new general government are found in Ajzenstat, Romney, Gentles, and Gairnder, ed., *Canada's Founding Debates*, chapter 3.

For the Alberta press case, see *Reference Re Alberta Statutes*, [1938] 2 S.C.R. 100.

CHAPTER NINE

"The whole apple cart." Let me be clear. The right of revolution is not about changing the political party in office. It's not about clearing out the old political gang and putting in a new one. It's not about repealing old laws and passing new ones. It's about changing the *constitution*. Changing the foundational laws and principles. Changing the *regime*. The Glorious Revolution of 1688 abolished the divine right of kings. The American Revolution made a new nation. Lockean revolutions change the deepest stratum, the bedrock foundations. It would be a Lockean revolution – the Lockean revolution par excellence – if the people were to reject all forms of government and all foundations to return to an anarchic "state of nature." See Locke's *Second Treatise of Government*, chapter XIX, "Of the Dissolution of Government."

How much publicity preceded the ratification of the Constitution Act, 1982? Though romantic democrats of the period sometimes argued that the 1982 act was entirely the work of the "men in suits," that is, the leaders of Canada's eleven governments, it is important to note that there had been decades of debate on constitutional change in the public arena and in federal-provincial meetings. In the two years preceding ratification, the opposition parties at both levels of government had their say in the legislatures and in the media and groups of concerned citizens appeared before the committees of the federal Parliament. Alan Cairns was the first political scientist to draw our attention to the consequences of popular involvement in the process of making the Constitution Act, 1982.

The Supreme Court of Canada approved the process that led to the 1982 act in the patriation reference of 1981 (*Attorney General of Manitoba et al,* v. *Attorney General of Canada et al.*) in the Supreme Court of Canada on 28 September 1981. See Peter Russell's *Constitutional Odyssey* (Toronto: University of Toronto Press 1992) for the process of drafting and rejecting the Meech and Charlottetown accords. Another helpful work on the constitutional process is David Milne, *The Canadian Constitution: From Patriation to Meech Lake* (Toronto: James Lorimer 1989).

The "absent sovereign" in U.S. constitutionalism. For a difficult but rewarding discussion, see Keith E. Whittington, *Constitutional Interpretation: Textual Meaning, Original Intent, and Judicial Review* (Lawrence, Kansas: University Press of Kansas 1991), Chapter 5. The phrase "absent sovereign" occurs at 154ff.

Parliament, when it meets, doesn't speak only for the party that won the last election. (Of course not!) It doesn't speak only for the electorate. It speaks for everyone who is bound by the law and everyone who benefits from the law.

The argument is that a decision reached by the deliberation of free members in an arena that in law and by tradition represents all the inhabitants of the country is superior to a verdict delivered by legislators tied by referendum to the majority in their province or constituency. Parliamentary ratification will necessarily have the form of a majority decision but it will more closely represent the will of the sovereign people.

Quotations from the legislative debates on Confederation in this section and the next are taken from Janet Ajzenstat, Paul Romney, Ian Gentles, and William D. Gairdner, ed., *Canada's Founding Debates* (Toronto: Stoddart, 1999; reissued by University of Toronto Press 2003), chapters 11 and 12.

Philip Buckner argues that opposition to Confederation in the Maritimes has perhaps been exaggerated: Buckner, "The Maritimes and Confederation: A Reassessment," *Canadian Historical Review* 81:1 (1990). But see the responses to Buckner that follow in the same issue of the *Review*.

On parliamentary protection of rights, Jean-Louis de Lolme, *The Constitution of England*, 1776, was my first guide. De Lolme argues that political parties compete for the privilege of extending the rights of the people. What better way to prove one's fitness to take the reigns of government than to discover the governing party in the act of transgressing rights? What better way to prove one's fitness to continue in office than to champion civil rights?

For (comparatively) recent statements that echo de Lolme, see Donald Smiley, *Canada in Question: Federalism in the Eighties*, 3rd edition (Toronto: McGraw-Hill Ryerson 1980), 42: the Fathers of Confederation intended the "protection of human rights to rest on the traditional safeguards of the civil and common law systems as these safeguards were from time to time modified by enactments of Parliament and the provincial legislatures." And see also Peter W. Hogg, *Constitutional Law of Canada*, 3rd edition (student edition) (Scarborough, Ont.: Carswell 1992): "Democracy is without doubt the most important safeguard of civil liberties." The entire passage is worth noting: "Canada's record [on civil liberties], while far from perfect, seems to be much better than that of most of the countries of the world, although nearly all countries have bills of rights in their constitutions. The basic reason for this has very little to do with the contents of Canada's (or any other country's) constitutional law. It is to be found in the democratic character of Canada's political institutions, supported by long traditions of free elections, opposition parties and a free press." And see Janet Ajzenstat, "Reconciling Parliament and Rights: A.V. Dicey Reads the Canadian Charter of Rights and Freedoms," *Canadian Journal of Political Science* 30:4 (1997).

CHAPTER TEN

For the scholars of right-centre-left, abstractions like "democracy," "equality," "individualism," and "community" enjoy an independent existence. They're history's heroes, the movers and shakers. They come into being, change the face of nations, lend their names to centuries and regimes. And when they pass away, their passing is cause for celebration or mourning. People, in contrast, are little more than background, or, it might be better to say, occasions for the expression and transmission of ideas. Consider C.B. Macpherson's *The Life and Times of Liberal Democracy* (Oxford: Oxford University Press 1977). The title says everything. *Life and Times*: the biography of an idea.

Horowitz writes: "The complete ideological spectrum ranges – in chronological order, and from right to left – from feudal or tory through liberal whig to liberal democrat to socialist." See

"Conservatism, Liberalism, and Socialism in Canada: An Interpretation," *Canadian Journal of Economics and Political Science* 32:2 (1966). And see Louis Hartz, *The Liberal Tradition in America* (New York: Harcourt, Brace and World 1955), and Hartz et al., *The Founding of New Societies* (New York: Harcourt, Brace and World 1964).

According to the r-c-l theorists, socialism is the culmination of the march of ideologies. But socialism is likely to arise only in Europe, because only Europe had the benefit of living through the feudal Middle Ages. Only Europe had the opportunity to stoke up enough conservative "karma" to generate full-blown socialism.

Among the scholars who have contributed to the new paradigm in American historiography are J.G.A. Pocock, *The Machiavellian Moment* (Princeton, N.J.: Princeton University Press 1975); Bernard Bailyn, *The Ideological Origins of the American Revolution* (Cambridge, Mass.: Harvard University Press 1967); and Gordon Wood, *The Creation of the American Republic, 1776–1782* (New York: Norton 1969). For a fuller bibliography, see Peter J. Smith's notes in "The Ideological Origins of Canadian Confederation," which first appeared in the *Canadian Journal of Political Science* in 1987. He was one of the first Canadian scholars to use the new paradigm to describe Canadian political history. His seminal article is reprinted in Janet Ajzenstat and Peter J. Smith, ed., *Canada's Origins: Liberal, Tory, or Republican?* (Ottawa: Carleton University Press 1995).

Keith Whittington assesses the new scholarship in *Constitutional Interpretation: Textual Meaning, Original Intent, and Judicial Review* (Lawrence: University Press of Kansas 1999), 228n36. For Michael Sandel's opinion, see "The Political Theory of the Procedural Republic," in Allan C. Hutchinson and Patrick Monahan ed., *The Rule of Law, Ideal or Ideology?* (Toronto: Carswell 1987). And for Taylor's appreciation of Sandel's view, see "Alternative Futures: Legitimacy, Identity, and Alienation in Late Twentieth-Century Canada," in Charles Taylor, *Reconciling the Solitudes*, ed. Guy Laforest (Montreal: McGill-Queen's University Press 1993).

CHAPTER ELEVEN

A popular graduate course at McMaster, taught jointly by the Department of Religion and the Department of Political Science, is entitled "Critics of Modernity." Probing the deficiencies of liberalism is high on the agenda. There is no course on the defenders of modernity. Such a program would not appeal to the critical academic intellect. And it might prove difficult to draw up a reading list! In this vein, see Ronald Beiner *What's the Matter with Liberalism?* (Berkeley: University of California Press 1992).

Lament for a Nation: The Defeat of Canadian Nationalism was first published in 1965 and has remained an academic best-seller since. The most recent copy in my collection was published in the Carleton Library Series (Ottawa: Carleton University Press 1995).

Of Grant's other works, I recommend two essays especially: "Faith and the Multiversity," in Grant, *Technology and Justice* (Toronto: Anansi 1986); and "In Defence of North America," in Grant, *Technology and Empire* (Toronto: Anansi 1969). The books and articles exploring his work are many. I'll mention only one: Yusuf K. Umar, ed., *George Grant and the Future of Canada* (Calgary: University of Calgary Press 1992). And see William Christian, *George Grant, A Biography* (Toronto: University of Toronto Press 1993). Grant died in 1988; editions of his unpublished essays and letters are still appearing. On "the universal and homogeneous state," see Leo Strauss, *On Tyranny, including the Strauss-Kojève Correspondence,* ed. Victor Gourevitch and Michael S. Roth (New York: The Free Press 1963).

Kenneth McRae argues that United Empire Loyalists were American liberals in Louis Hartz, ed., *The Founding of New Societies* (New York: Harcourt, Brace and World 1964). Barry Cooper argues that Canada's political philosophers, not least Hartz and Horowitz, typically ignore the provinces of western and eastern Canada, ascribing national significance to the history and concerns of Ontario and Quebec. See, for example, his "Western Political Consciousness," in Stephen Brooks, ed., *Political Thought in Canada* (Toronto: Irwin 1984). But what are we to say about the romanticism of the phenomenon dubbed "western separatism"? Are there romantics in Canada's Atlantic provinces, the west, the north? Of course. Fierce loyalty to particular regions, coupled with resentment at being left out by the prevailing "typologies" of the Canadian heartland: the posture may be contradictory, but it is the kind of contradiction that appeals to the romantic imagination.

To long for something one can't have, or can no longer have, is the essence of romance. In Georges Bizet's *The Pearl Fishers*, the priestess and the pearl fisher reveal their love for each other on a starlit beach in ancient Ceylon. As the curtain rises, the audience gasps: the ruins of great temples dwarf the singers; a glowing sea stretches away. Ancient ruins, endless sea, heaven bending towards earth! This is romance! But do the lovers celebrate their surroundings? No. As their passions rise, they sing about the delicious nights of years before in "the perfumed forest" when he first heard her singing and she first knew he was listening. The feelings they express in their soaring song are not those they feel as they embrace on the beach, but those they knew when they had barely glimpsed each other and had not yet embraced: *that's* romance.

Judith Shklar is helpful on the despair of the late romantics: *After Utopia: The Decline of Political Faith* (Princeton, N.J.: Princeton University Press 1957). And see Shklar on the romantic's horror at technology and disdain for the masses, in *After Utopia*, Chapter 4, especially page 113.

No one reading Grant can fail to benefit from his analysis of moral and religious issues; a profound vision of our relation to God informs his writing. But admirable as it is, or perhaps exactly because it is so elevated, this glorious moral teaching turns to lead when translated into a prescription for Canadian democracy.

The strange thing is that Grant's disciples agree with him on very little. They want a forward-looking, progressive country, not the conservative, deferential one he described. They ignore his penchant for oligarchy; they reject his teaching on religion and politics. Nevertheless, they continue to think of him as their teacher. Canadian nationhood had been "our own," our precious inheritance. We had lost it. Surely we could summon something like it again.

The "economic nationalists" are prominent among Grant's interpreters and disciples. They were dedicated to combating free trade and all forms of economic integration with the United States. Well-known members of this school are James Laxer, Kari Levitt, Ian Lumsden, W.H. Pope, Abraham Rotstein, Phillipe Syke, and John W. Warnock. Their legacy can be seen today at the "economic summits" where Canadian youngsters (and some people not so young!) burn American flags and battle the police.

The "cultural nationalists" argue for regulations to curtail the influence of American arts and artists.

CHAPTER TWELVE

For Trudeau's essays on nationalism, especially "New Treason of the Intellectuals" and "Federalism, Nationalism and Reason," see Pierre Elliott Trudeau, *Federalism and the French Canadians* (Toronto: Macmillan, Laurentian Library 1968).

As I argued in the sources section of Chapter 1, Canadians at one time looked to institutions rather than culture as the source of identity. They described themselves as the subjects or citizens of a parliamentary regime, enjoying the security for rights and freedoms offered by the British rule-of-law tradition. Trudeau undoubtedly intended the institutional reforms of the Constitution Act, 1982 to define Canadian nationhood. But the result of his reforms was to undermine further the old confidence in Parliament and the rule of law. A good essay showing that the Charter has not contributed markedly to national unity can be found in Rainer Knopff and F.L. Morton, *Charter Politics* (Scarborough, Ont.: Nelson Canada 1992).

Many political scientists and lawyers argue that, with the introduction of the Charter of Rights and Freedoms, the Canadian courts have moved from the "penumbra of political power to its bright core." Some approve of this development; some are wary. Knopff and Morton's books are a good introduction. They themselves fall squarely on the side of the "wary." See their *Charter Politics*, and F.L. Morton and Rainer Knopff, *The Charter Revolution and the Court Party* (Peterborough, Ont.: Broadview Press 2000).

I am indebted to Judith Shklar for descriptions of the German champion of ethnic particularity, Herder, whom she calls "the first truly romantic thinker." See Shklar, *After Utopia: The Decline of Political Faith* (Princeton, N.J.: Princeton University Press 1957), 12ff., 16, and elsewhere.

Who are the Canadian romantic nationalists? James Tully is one. See Tully, *Strange Multiplicity: Constitutionalism in an Age of Diversity* (Cambridge, U.K.: Cambridge University Press 1995), 197: "... cultural recognition is a deep and abiding human need." The argument continues: "The suppression of cultural differences in the name of uniformity and unity is one of the leading causes of civil strife, disunity and dissolution today." According to Tully, it's liberalism that's chiefly responsible for the suppression of differences. Liberal democracy in the classic definition is intolerant, repressive, and imperialistic. Its arguments are inadequate and its practices cruel.

There's a signal difference between Grant's disciples (the economic and cultural nationalists) and the romantic nationalists. The former are always struggling to describe the Canadian and American ways of life and to pin down Canadian-American differences. The romantics, in contrast, shy away from precise description and seldom compare cultures. They analyse liberalism in the course of arguing that it is incompatible with cultural diversity, but they say little about other regimes and other ways of life except that it's essential to preserve them. Their reluctance to describe cultures is perhaps understandable. It's considered impolite these days to write about someone else's culture. It's "voice appropriation."

Consider Patrick Macklem, *Indigenous Difference and the Canadian Constitution* (Toronto: University of Toronto Press 2001). Macklem argues that indigenous rights trump all other rights in Canada. The distinctive way(s) of life enjoyed by Canada's First Nations ought to be preserved in the face of all countervailing political claims. This is a very strong contention; non-aboriginal Canadians might be curious about the characteristics of the aboriginal ways they are committing themselves to respect and maintain. But Macklem says nothing on this score. He does not show us the different ways and does not argue that those ways of life are good, or superior. He says merely that other Canadians must respect them and preserve them, even at the expense, if necessary, of their own perceived interests.

In arguments for aboriginal nationhood, it's sometimes suggested that the aboriginal way is superior because aboriginals are more community-oriented than run-of-the-mill Canadians. But since those who put forward such arguments usually believe that run-of-the-mill Canadians are *supposed* to be community-oriented, such statements do not convey a concrete idea of cultural difference. The First Nations live up to the ideal; most Canadians don't. What kind of cultural difference is being described? Many people believe that the First Nations care more for the environment. But, of course, non-aboriginals ought to care for the environment too.

A celebrated source for the defence of the "situated self" is Michael Sandel. See his criticisms of John Rawls in the Introduction to *Liberalism and Its Critics* ed. Michael Sandel (New York: New York University Press 1984). John Rawls's description of liberalism in *A Theory of Justice* (Boston: Harvard University Press 1971) provoked, in response, the school of political thought called communitarianism. Sandel is a central figure in this school. As I suggested in the sources section of the last chapter, Sandel comes to identify communitarianism with the ideology called by J.G.A. Pocock and Peter J. Smith "civic republicanism."

Charles Taylor's essays on Canada, written at different times and for different purposes, have been collected and edited by Guy Laforest. See Taylor, *Reconciling the Solitudes: Essays on Canadian Federalism and Nationalism*, ed Guy Laforest (Montreal: McGill-Queen's University Press 1993).

Some of the issues in this section are thrashed out in *Multiculturalism and "The Politics of Recognition": An Essay by Charles Taylor*, ed. Amy Gutman with commentary by Amy Gutmann, Steven C. Rockefeller, Michael Walzer, and Susan Wolf (Princeton, N.J.: Princeton University Press 1992). The authors address the crucial question raised by George Grant as well as Taylor: Can a democratic society treat all its members as equals and also recognize their specific cultural identities?

See Pierre Elliott Trudeau, *Conversation with Canadians* (Toronto: University of Toronto Press 1972), and Jeremy Webber, *Reimagining Canada: Language, Culture, Community, and the Canadian Constitution* (Montreal: McGill-Queen's University Press 1994). The argument that identities are the product of conversation is developed in Chapter 6, "Language, Culture, and Political Community."

Ordinary mission statements are just pious assertions. A constitutional preamble like that proposed for Charlottetown would have been open to adjudication in the courts and might thus have had real political clout, making it something worth fighting over. I think that the Fathers of Confederation would agree with Webber on one point: ambitious statements about a nation's goals and values are inappropriate in a constitution. They didn't include such statements in the 1867 document for good reason.

James Tully offers an argument about identity not unlike Webber's. In the striking image that lies at the heart of his book, he asks us to think of the various cultures of a multicultural society as squabbling, jostling passengers in a tippy canoe. The image is drawn from Haida myth, and inspired by Bill Reid's famous sculpture, *The Black Canoe*. Some of the creatures in Reid's sculpture are frightening in appearance – bears and wolves; only some are human or mostly human. All speak or vocalize all the time – they converse – each in his or her language, "telling their diverse stories and claims." At the same time, they all keep paddling, and – most wonderful – the canoe moves steadily forward. According to Tully, the tippy canoe is the just constitution, and the squabbling is the sound of peoples engaged in a dialogue or "multilogue" in which each constantly asserts, negotiates, and renegotiates its cultural identity. See Tully, *Strange Multiplicity*.

There are two puzzling features of Tully's description of *The Black Canoe*. According to Tully, the creatures lack a common language. Yet they all understand each other. They "exchange stories." They "see their common and interwoven histories come together from a multiplicity of paths." Tully supposes that there is no common language because he wishes to say that in the just constitution there will be no "meta-narrative"; a common language or meta-narrative is liberal and imperialistic. He suggests at one point that it's the chief who explains each creature to the others. But the presence of the chief raises the second puzzling question. In Reid's sculpture, the chief is huge, crowned, dominant, looming over the others. Can Tully be saying that the culturally diverse society of the future will stay afloat only if ruled by a tyrant – or supernatural being?

Patrick Macklem, *Indigenous Difference and the Constitution of Canada*, also regards identities as the product of dialogue. James Tully is one of his authorities. But Macklem would exclude certain groups from the conversation, and he believes that the Canadian courts can and should end dialogue at a certain point. He is highly unfriendly to the argument for gender equality in the determination of band membership and argues that the courts should protect from Charter scrutiny the provisions of the Indian Act that allow only members of the band councils to say who belongs and who doesn't.

CHAPTER THIRTEEN

"A man may be allowed to keep Poisons": Jonathan Swift, *Gulliver's Travels*, Part Two, Chapter 6. The King of Brobdingnag is speaking to Gulliver. "He said he knew no reason why those who entertain Opinions prejudicial to the Publick should be obliged to change, or should not be obliged to conceal them. And as it was Tyranny in any Government to require the first, so it was Weakness not to enforce the second: For a man may be allowed to keep Poisons. ..."

"To submit to politics was an act of resigning to actuality and as such an abandonment of romanticism." See Judith Shklar, *After Utopia: The Decline of Political Faith* (Princeton, N.J.: Princeton University Press 1957), 107. "That group romanticism was eventually put to the service of ordinary politics was the last of the many self-inflicted defeats of romanticism."

"How are men to be reconciled with each other?" For Berlin on Schiller, see *The Roots of Romanticism* (Princeton, N.J.: Princeton University Press 1999), 86.

Can one mode of thinking embrace both extreme individualism and cultural immersion? Aren't these notions inherently in tension? It's a dilemma. Reg Whitaker notes a similar one (or it may be the same one). He finds in Canada today two new and "radically incompatible narratives: *identity politics* and *populism*." (It's part of his argument that "identity politics" and "populism" are replacing the "old narratives" – conservatism, liberalism, and socialism. He has a point!) Reg Whitaker, "Canadian Politics at the End of the Millennium: Old Dreams, New Nightmares," in David Taras and Beverly Rasporich, eds., *A Passion for Identity: An Introduction to Canadian Studies* (Scarborough, Ont.: Nelson 1997). Let's think about Whitaker's suggestion that identity politics and populism are incompatible. I would argue that they are – from the Enlightenment perspective. The question is whether they are incompatible from the romantic point of view. Indeed, the question is whether the word "incompatible" doesn't lose its power in romanticism's wild wood.

In the sources section of Chapter 2, I said that Irshad Manji searches for a political prescription to reconcile individuality and community: *Risking Hope: On the Edge of a New Democracy* (Toronto:

Douglas and McIntyre 1997). She wants modes of individual expression that will "build" community. But what her book supremely does is to tell the stories of young people (herself, and women and men she interviews in a journey across Canada) who fail to reconcile passionate assertions of individuality with communal demands. Or often fail; I cannot say that they always fail. As the commentator on the back cover (the pollster Michael Adams) says, their attempts result in "joy and pain." To understand why attempts to reconcile individuality and community seem so necessary and so desirable and yet yield pain, we would have to move beyond Manji to French philosophy, beginning with the master, Jean Jacques Rousseau. Rousseau argues that to live in the opinion of others, to see oneself in and through the reactions and attitudes of others, disposes one to suffer, and, note, disposes one to perform cruel acts.

The "essence of the romantic movement, so far as I can see [is] will and man as an activity": Berlin, *The Roots of Romanticism*, 138. "When he looked within himself as people normally do ..." (Fichte on the self): Berlin, *The Roots of Romanticism*, 93.

"A peculiar situation has arisen": see Berlin, *The Roots of Romanticism*, 146. On Berlin's ambiguities, see Mark Lilla, Ronald Dworkin, and Robert B. Silvers, *The Legacy of Isaiah Berlin* (New York: New York Review Books 2001), especially the article by Lilla, "Wolves and Lambs," and the exchange between Aileen Kelly, Mark Lilla, and Steven Lukes, 59–69. Lilla rejects the assertion that liberalism was originally monist. It's Lilla's argument that liberalism was born of the desire to accommodate pluralism and to find the institutions that will support it while curtailing its destructive contestations in the public realm. Thus, in Lilla's opinion, and in mine, it's not a coincidence that today the most tolerant and most pluralistic nations are Canada, the United States, and other enclaves around the world that acknowledge Locke's influence.

CHAPTER FOURTEEN

"History from below": the phrase is Alan Cairns's. History from below is a feature of American universities as well as Canadian. Indeed, it's sometimes called "the new international historiography." Or the "new social history." See Jack Granatstein, *Who Killed Canadian History?* (Toronto: HarperCollins 1998).

I suggested in the sources section of Chapter 1 that political scientists, with some notable exceptions, turned to economics and sociology in the 1960s. Study of law, legislatures, and the constitution was not abandoned entirely, but the assumption grew up that these institutions were "epiphenomenal," the product of social and economic factors. Thus, to understand the Canadian way of life, one looked at patterns of immigration, economic developments, and "culture" rather than parliamentary institutions, surety for rights, and other features of liberal democracy. It was even said by some that federalism is a function of social factors. One of the best introductions to the issue is still the first chapter of Donald Smiley's *Canada in Question: Federalism in the Eighties*, 3rd ed. (Toronto: McGraw-Hill Ryerson 1980). Smiley asks: "Does Society decisively determine Government – or is it the other way round?" I don't want to engage the issue here. I want to note merely that Smiley thought the sociological argument strong enough to require careful rebuttal. To make it, he drew on Alan Cairns's 1977 presidential address to the Canadian Political Science Association. Smiley's conviction that one can't discount the influence of government has been given a boost in recent years by the school of "neo-institutionalism," which, not surprising, also draws on Cairns. Nevertheless, the fascination with the idea that "society determines" is still with us. It's the view that supports our "buttoned up" definition of the Canadian identity.

Cairns describes changing attitudes to the Canadian constitution in "The Other Crisis of Canadian Federalism," an essay first published in 1977. See *Constitution, Government, and Society in Canada, Selected Essays by Alan C. Cairns*, ed. Douglas E. Williams (Toronto: McClelland and Stewart 1988), chapter 6.

The Charlottetown Accord amended the Constitution Act, 1867, the Constitution Act 1982, and some other constitutional documents. The Consensus Report, Final Text (August 1992) and the Draft Legal Text (October 1992) can be found in Kenneth McRoberts and Patrick Monahan, ed., *The Charlottetown Accord, the Referendum, and the Future of Canada* (Toronto: University of Toronto Press 1993). The volume includes articles by political scientists and Charlottetown activists (some showing the scars of their defeat), as well as the referendum results by province. And see Curtis Cook, ed., *Constitutional Predicament: Canada after the Referendum of 1992* (Montreal: McGill-Queen's University Press 1994). As Mark Charleton and Paul Barker note in *Crosscurrents: Contemporary Political Issues*, 3rd ed. (Toronto: Nelson 1998), there is a huge literature on the reform process from 1982 to 1992. They offer a selected bibliography. We abandoned the study of constitutional law in the 1960s when it would have been helpful. We returned to it in the 1980s. Better late than never?

The Reform Party, the Communist Party, and the National Party were among the organizations that called for a New Canada. Think about the National Party's use of this slogan. What kind of nationalism calls for a new country? (Answer: a Canadian nationalism, of course.)

On the participation of groups in constitution making, see Alan Cairns, "The Politics of Constitutionalism," in Keith Banting and Richard Simeon, ed., *Federalism, Democracy and the Constitution Act*, (Toronto: Methuen 1983); and Cairns, "Ottawa, the Provinces and Meech Lake," in Roger Gibbins et al., ed., *Meech Lake and Canada: Perspectives from the West* (Edmonton: Academic 1988). I should list Cairns's books, which are chiefly collections of his essays, but I'll leave it to the reader to discover them for herself.

Many political scientists writing about constitutional reform are activists. Robert Jackson writes: "When I was a young student at Oxford we had two types of speaker. There were analysts and specimens. The specimens were the politicians, who were analysed like insects – put under a microscope. These are the people who were on the Yes and No sides of the referendum campaign. The analysts were the professors who came to study the politicians or activists. On this topic [the Charlottetown Accord], I am a specimen, and I regard most Canadian political scientists as being specimens as well. In fact, I was quite surprised to hear at this conference that there are a few people in Canada commenting on the question of the constitution who do not seem to be specimens." For other articles from the conference Jackson mentions, see Curtis Cook, ed., *Constitutional Predicament*; for his remarks, see 127.

The Canada clause, section 2 (1), (a) to (h) of the Draft Legal

Text of October 1992, affirms the importance of Canada's parliamentary and federal institutions and the rule of law, the rights of aboriginals, Quebec's distinct society, the vitality of the official-language minority communities throughout Canada, racial and ethnic identity, respect for individual and collective rights, the equality of male and female persons, and the equality of the provinces "at the same time as recognizing their diverse characteristics." (What's your opinion? Is the clause a heart-warming assertion of our nation's values? Or a dog's breakfast?)

"The sporadic desire for self-expression": in this passage, Judith Shklar is writing about the years after the Second World War. "The participation, and the subsequent disillusion with, totalitarian movements has reinforced the unhappy consciousness." Yet the "Byronic impulse is by no means dead." See Shklar, *After Utopia: The Decline of Political Faith* (Princeton, N.J.: Princeton University Press 1957), 145.

An end to poverty: see part Part III of the Charlottetown Accord, Draft Legal Text, The Social and Economic Union. It commits Canadian governments to the provision of adequate social services, comprehensive health care, high-quality primary and secondary education, and so on. These goals are not "justiciable," that is, not open to enforcement by the courts. The argument for a justiciable charter of social and economic rights is still alive in academic circles.

For an academic piece on the lines of the Gilbert-and-Sullivan philosophy, see Ian Brodie, "The Market for Political Status," *Comparative Politics* 28 (1996), 253–71. On the politics of the apolitical, see Shklar, *After Utopia*, 145.

Peter Russell's contention that elites in 1990 were still unwilling to consult the people on constitutional reform is found in *Constitutional Odyssey: Canadians Be a Sovereign People?* (Toronto: University of Toronto Press 1992). Evidence to support the idea that elites responded to the people can be found in Janet Ajzenstat, "Constitution Making and the Myth of the People, in *Constitutional Predicament*, ed. Curtis Cook, and in some books and articles listed above in this chapter.

The Canada West Foundation argued that "constitutional reform is too important to leave to the regular partisan-dominated political process." Cited in John Dafoe, "Assembly idea has seized the political imagination," *Globe and Mail*, 6 July 1991, D2.

Keith Spicer called for a "manifestly non-partisan" constitutional constituent assembly. See "Chairman's Foreword," *Citizens' Forum on Canada's Future: Report to the People and Government of Canada* (the Spicer Report) (Ottawa: Supply and Services 1991), 5. That "dialogue" among "non-politicians" would be more productive than meetings of elected representatives was argued at length in *Maclean's* magazine in July 1991, 10–76. With the help of Decima Research, the magazine chose twelve Canadians to represent the dominant lines of thinking on the constitutional crisis. Conflict experts from Harvard University presided over a weekend meeting of these representative citizens, described by *Maclean's* as a model for resolving Canada's constitution-making crisis. One participant summed up the group's feeling: "Let's get the politicians out of it."

The majority report of the Beaudoin-Edwards Committee, which argued for ratification of constitutional amendments by Parliament and the provincial legislatures was swimming against the tide. See *The Process for Amending the Constitution of Canada: The Report of the Special Joint Committee of the Senate and the House of Commons* (Beaudoin-Edwards Report), 20 June 1991.

"The parliamentary process ... is the antithesis of a process that not only hears all voices but takes all experiences and aspirations into account": Donna Greschner, "Commentary," in David E. Smith, Peter MacKinnon, and John C. Courtney, ed., *After Meech Lake* (Saskatoon: Fifth House 1991), 224. And see other essays in this volume.

One feels some alarm at the suggestion embodied in the Spicer Report that Canadians want stronger political leaders, leaders with "vision and courage," who will not "govern by the polls or play sterile partisan games." *Citizens' Forum on Canada's Future*, 8. This is the language of romantic totalitarianism.

Index

aboriginal nationhood, 138, 180
American Civil War, 71
American constitution: as form of mixed government, 76; John A. Macdonald praises, 170; romantic perceptions of, 42, 170
American president: as head of state and head of government, 169
American Revolution, 16, 27, 137
Annand, William (Nova Scotia House of Assembly), 85
Aristotle: on citizenship, 8; on mixed government, 72, 135

Bailyn, Bernard, 101
Baldwin, Robert, 48, 163
Barber, Benjamin, 159
Beattie, Owen, 157
Bédard, Pierre, 34, 44, 74; on responsible government, 49–50
Beiner, Ronald, 104
Berlin, Isaiah, 9, 153; on Fichte and romanticism, 131–2, 134; on the origins of totalitarianism, 22, 158; on Schiller, 129
Bernstein, Leonard, 132
Bizet, Georges, 178
Blaikie, Bill, 47
Bloom, Allan, 159
British North America Act, 40; and money bills, 65–6; and political equality, 55; and responsible government, 66–7; the "similar in principle" clause, 79. *See also* Constitution Act, 1867
Bronfman Foundation ("historical minute"), 166
Brown, George, 72; on the appointive Senate, 77
Buckner, Phillip: on the Canadian Fathers and democracy, 59, 61, 63, 70, 169; on the origins of responsible government, 50
Burke, Edmund: on instruction of legislators, 84
Byron, Lord, 161, 163

Cairns, Alan C., 173, 184–6
Campbell, Stewart (Nova Scotia House of Assembly), 86
Canadian national identity: and anti-Americanism, 112–13, 116; and history, 6. *See also* ideological continuum
Carter, F.B.T. (Newfoundland House of Assembly): on mixed government, 75
Cartier, George-Étienne: on the American constitution, 170; on populist democracy, 70–1, 126
Cauchon, Joseph (Canadian Legislative Assembly), 83
Charlottetown Conference of 1864, 55
Charlottetown Constitutional Accord of 1991, 82, 138; and the

Index

Canada clause, 140, 186–7; and popular sovereignty, 142–4, 145–6
Chateau Clique, 6, 165
civic republicanism, 8, 9, 108; in American historiography, 100–1. *See also* Smith, Peter J.
Confederation debates: in the colonial legislatures, 55–6
Constitution Act, 1867: and money bills, 68
Constitution Act, 1982, 81–2

De Lolme, Jean-Louis, 74, 174–5; on political equality, 172
Dorion, A.-A. (Canadian Legislative Assembly), 170
Duff, Chief Justice Lyman Poore: on liberal democracy in the British North America Act, 95; opinion in the Alberta press case, 78–80
Durham, Lord, 165–6; on money bills and responsible government, 48–9, 65–6, 165; on political equality, 51; on property rights, 62; on the romantics, 49

economic nationalism, 101, 112, 116, 178

Family Compact, 6, 99
franchise: in British North America, 61; in England, 40, 61; extension of, 133
Frost, Robert, 34, 160–1

Gairdner, William D., 154
Gilbert, William (New Brunswick House of Assembly), 56
Glorious Revolution of 1688, 16, 27; and political equality, 51; and popular sovereignty, 53; and responsible government, 40, 48
Granatstein, Jack, 137
Grant, George, 99, 151; on Lockean liberalism, 106–7; moral teaching, 178; political legacy, 112–13
Greschner, Donna, 156

Hartz, Louis, 94, 97–8; on political deliberation in the United States, 113. *See also* ideological continuum
Hobbes, Thomas, 133, 158; on natural equality, 57
Hogg, Peter, 175
Horowitz, Gad, 93–5, 97–9; on liberal democracy, 175; on political deliberation in Canada, 113
Howe, Joseph, 43; mentioned in Confederation debates as defender of Red River settlers, 87

ideological continuum (right-centre-left), 11–13, 73, 93–4, 175; in Canadian textbooks, 18; and historical determinism, 7, 13, 71–2; and limits on political deliberation, 7, 8, 113–15

individualism: and community, 16, 20, 129, 131–2, 155; fostered by public dialogue, 124–5, 126, 182–3. *See also* romanticism

Jackson, Robert, 186
Johnson, John Mercer (New Brunswick House of Assembly), 57

Kojève, Alexandre, 106
Kymlicka, Will, 123

Laird, Alexander (Prince Edward Island House of Assembly), 87
Lawrence, William (Nova Scotia House of Assembly), 56
Lessing, Doris, 157
liberal democracy: Canadian academics do not befriend, 103, 105
Locke, John, 127, 133; in the American founding, 100; in the Canadian founding, 8, 54, 81, 156; on natural equality, 51; and political deliberation, 153; on popular sovereignty, 28, 56, 58, 88; on the right of revolution, 173; on security for rights, 76; on separation of church and state, 23, 158; on the state of nature, 53

MacDiarmid, Hugh, 157
Macdonald, John A., 99, 126; on democracy, 71; on mixed govern-

Index

ment, 75; on rights of minorities, 68
Mackenzie, William Lyon, 28
Macklem, Patrick, 180, 182
McLelan, Archibald (Nova Scotia House of Assembly), 86
McMaster University: George Grant's lectures at, 109; graduate course on the critics of modernity, 176
Macpherson, C.B., 96–7, 175; and romantic democracy, 157; and romanticism, 102
McRae, Kenneth, 108, 152
Malcolmson, Patrick, 89
Manji, Irshad, 155, 183
Meech Lake Accord of 1987, 82, 145
mixed government, 72–3, 75; and absolutism, 135–6; in the American constitution, 76; in the Canadian Parliament, 64, 67, 74, 76, 77; and natural equality, 74, 75; and political deliberation, 78; and the upper chamber, 74–5. See also separation of constitutional powers
Montesquieu, 73, 74, 93
Moore, Christopher, 163–4, 168
Mowat, Oliver, 72
multiculturalism: in Canada and in the United States, 120; and the Canadian political identity, 114; and political equality, 127

National Election Survey (NES), 14, 16
national identity: constrains political deliberation, 7, 5, 113–15; determined by public dialogue, 124–5, 141–2; political determinants of, 58, 185; social determinants of, 185
National Policy: of John A. Macdonald, 89, 94

O'Halloran, James (Canadian Legislative Assembly), 56
oligarchy: in British North America, 42–3; George Grant's defence of, 107–8. See also Family Compact, Chateau Clique
Ouellet, Fernand, 161–2

Papineau, Louis-Joseph, 13, 28, 49, 71
Parent, Étienne, 43
Parizeau, Jacques, 110
parliamentary reform, 155, 164
Peace, Order, and Good Government, 16, 128, 156
political contestation: in liberal-democratic theory, 11, 16–17, 46, 69, 89. See also political deliberation
political deliberation: John A. Macdonald on, 84; in liberal-democratic theory, 17, 36, 46, 98; in Parliament, 52, 68; as security for rights, 88–9
political representation: and equality, 40; in

Parliament, 57, 169; and statistical sampling, 14, 46
popular sovereignty: and the Canadian founding, 52, 55, 56; and the Charlottetown Accord, 145–6; and Parliament, 57; and political equality, 52–3. See also Locke, John, on the right of revolution

Quebec: as distinct society, 140–1
Quebec Conference of 1864, 55–6

Rawls, John, 120–3
Rebellions of 1837–38, 28, 37
Rebick, Judy, 156–7
referendum, 15, 57; in constitution making, 84–6
religion and politics, 26, 108–9, 128. See also Locke, John, on separation of church and state
responsible government: in the British North America Act, 63, 67; and "cabinet oligarchy," 15, 46–7; and democracy, 40, 48; as defence against oligarchy, 68–9; in English history, 61; and regionalism, 45. See also Durham, Lord; Bédard, Pierre
right of revolution: in Canada and the United States, 81. See also Locke, John, and popular sovereignty

Roebuck, John Arthur, 49, 166
romanticism: as Canadian ideology, 12; and constitution making, 35, 139; and disdain for community, 103, 129; fosters community, 15, 130, 162; and individual fulfilment, 9, 15, 22, 121, 130; and nationalism, 118–19, 122, 141; and opposition to political engagement, 34, 38–9; origins, 22; on reconciling individualism and community, 129–30; and revolution, 28
Rousseau, Jean-Jacques, 13, 93, 162; on democracy and individual fulfilment, 9; on social dependency and cruelty, 184; on the state of nature, 54
Russell, Peter H., 53, 57–8

Salutin, Rick, 163

Sandel, Michael, 101, 160
Scruton, Roger, 159
separation of constitutional powers, 67; in the British constitution, 77; in Canada and in the United States, 76
Seymour, Benjamin (Canadian Legislative Council), 85
Shklar, Judith: on romantic engagement in politics, 128, 139; on totalitarianism, 22, 112, 158
Smiley, Donald, 175, 185
Smith, Peter J., 7–9, 108
street riots, 15, 33–4, 130, 178
Swift, Jonathan, 128

Taylor, Charles, 101, 122, 176
toleration of dissent: liberals on, 184; romantics on, 134. *See also* Locke, John, on separation of church and state
totalitarianism: liberals on, 135, 160; romantics on, 21–2, 35, 135
Trudeau, Pierre Elliott, 116–18, 123–4; on members of Parliament as "nobodies," 76; on political deliberation, 117
Tully, James, 135, 179–80, 182

United Empire Loyalists, 6, 89, 93–6, 107
upper chamber (Senate), 77–8; election of, 63, 77; and mixed government, 74, 75

Webber, Jeremy, 124–6, 131; compared to the Fathers on political deliberation, 181
Wetmore, William (New Brunswick House of Assembly), 85
Whitaker, Reg, 183
Whittington, Keith, 101
women: and political participation, 133
Wordsworth, William, 161